LXXXI—QUAREIA
THE MAGICIAN'S DECK

Cassandra Beanland, Stuart Littlejohn,
& Josephine McCarthy

A GUIDE TO THE
CARD MEANINGS

by Josephine McCarthy

SECOND EDITION

First published 2014
Second edition 2017

Published by Quareia Publishing UK

Typeset and copyedited by Michael Sheppard

Contents

X   Layouts   210

Introduction

The soul takes nothing with her to the next world but her education and her culture. At the beginning of the journey to the next world, one's education and culture can either provide the greatest assistance, or else act as the greatest burden, to the person who has just died.

— Plato, *The Republic*

LXXXI—Quareia The Magician's Deck is a unique magical tool for twenty-first century magicians. The deck has eighty-one cards, a mystical number that relates to completion, and it is divided into four realms: the *Divine Realm* (red borders), the *Inner Realm* (blue borders), the *Physical World* (green borders) and the *Realm of Death and the Underworld* (black borders). Cards which belong in two realms, or which are bridges between two realms, have borders containing both colours.

The Magician's Deck is not based on any tarot system, but rather it draws on the mythic, mystical, and magical powers that underpin the magical systems from which tarot eventually developed. It is based on real inner realms, real inner contacts, and beings and forces that the serious practitioner of magic is very likely to involve themselves with.

Because of this approach the deck works as a contacted deck, i.e. used magically the images can act as gateways to inner realms, inner beings, and magical patterns. It is not a deck for casual tarot readers; rather it is a deck specifically designed for magical students, practitioners, workers, and adepts working within the broad spectrum of Western magic. It can be used for magical divination or as a direct connection to inner contacts; as gateways for meditation, magical visionary work, soul exploration, or contacted ritual work. However it is important that the aspiring Initiate does not come to rely too much on such images as gateways: they are tools, along with many other tools that the magician employs on their path to mystical and magical development.

To ensure that the images do not become entangled in magical misconceptions we have moved away from the relatively modern use of particular names for the beings in the images. Instead we have reverted to a very ancient way of presenting inner beings:

we name them according to what they do. This way, there is no ambiguity about what a being actually is.

Magicians from most magical systems will recognize many if not all of the beings in this deck; not from their images, but from what they do, where they are from, and what power they operate through. This approach enables magicians and practitioners from many different magical and spiritual traditions to recognize the powers in this deck and to work with them within their own magical system.

The same theme runs through the two main layouts for the deck, in that each position tells its own story and has its own meaning. Reading the card and the layout position together, the magician can get a broad understanding of the answer to his or her question.

Introduction to the Second Edition

When *LXXXI—Quareia The Magician's Deck* was first produced, it was envisioned for Quareia students. At the time, we never thought that people outside of Quareia would be interested in such a niche deck. We were wrong!

As this book was originally designed for the use of Quareia Initiates and Adepts, many things were not explained or discussed, as there was no perceived need to. However, now we know differently. We have been surprised and pleased at the sheer volume of interest in *The Magician's Deck*, and as such, we realized that the book was not sufficiently fit for purpose.

This second edition has been expanded with more detail and with reference information for wider use in divination and magic. The deck can also be used with any layout that the reader understands, and for mundane as well as magical readings: the second edition of this book has been adjusted to reflect this wider use.

The Four Realms

The Four Realms reflect the four stages of creation and destruction. As such, they can be used magically to track a power or event: is it still forming? Is it coming into physical manifestation? Is it physically active? Is it passing into removal?

For mundane readings, the realms can represent the following pattern: an idea (Divine Realm), the development phase (Inner Realm), currently complete and active (Physical Realm), leaving or has died off (Underworld Realm). As we go through the book we will look at each realm in turn and investigate who the players are, what the powers are, and what they do.

The hour is ripe, and yonder lies the way.

— Virgil

Chapter I

The Divine Realm

It is precisely because there is nothing within the One that all things are from it.

— Plotinus

The Divine Realm is the place where no human can tread, living or dead, in dreams or in visions, but where only the powers of Divinity reside. This power flows across the expanse known to magicians as the Abyss and spills into the Inner Realm, before finally expressing in the physical world.

These cards appear when a Divine power is flowing into the creation or destruction of something. In mundane divination, the cards of this realm indicate deep, lasting powers behind events in the physical world and/or a person's life.

STAR FATHER I

Star Father
I

When the Star Father appears, it tells us that a new and as yet unformed potential of power is beginning to express itself. The cards that fall around it will tell us a bit about how this potential will manifest. It can mean a new life, a new path, and be as vast as a new civilization or as subtle as the seed for a personal revelation.

The use of the word 'Father' does not indicate gender; rather it refers to a power that seeks to 'output.' It is the first breath that crosses the divide, that flows into the lungs of the newborn, and the first utterance that creates.

The key to understanding this card is that the power is Divine: it is a vibration that moves towards creation which eventually manifests. It is the first spark, a sound that becomes 'the Word' or the first sliver of light in the darkness. The Star Father is the Divine Intention that seeks a new expression.

Mundane Divination: The very beginning of something before it becomes fully formed, the first step on a new path, the conception, an idea, the new direction, a new phase of something.

CREATOR OF TIME II

The Creator of Time
II

The Creator of Time is the Divine power that flows from the Star Father as it begins its journey into manifestation. It begins to form the pattern of life by taking the Divine Spark from pure light into life/manifestation: "the Light shone in the Darkness, and the Darkness comprehended it not." The light is Divine consciousness beginning to take form and pattern. It is the first step towards life, towards the weave that is our universe, and that first step is the creation of time.

The Creator of Time shows that a time line is forming for something new: the creation of time is woven into the pattern of manifestation by the Weaver of Creation, and it will eventually 4 8 pass into the hands of the Three Fates.

This card tells us that something is now taking form and becoming solidified, though it still has the potential to manifest in any number of ways. It is the pattern that forms time and substance. It is a powerful card, and its appearance tells us that deep and powerful creative powers are at work, and that a 'new time' is being formed for the subject of the reading. This new time heralds the creation of a new cycle of fate that will eventually express in a person's life. The card can also be read as literally 'adding time' to something.

Mundane Divination: Incubation, the formation of boundaries for a new beginning, a line of fate forming, a new fate path that has formed itself, the beginning of a new round of events, being given more time, a new period of time in which to accomplish something.

HOLDER OF LIGHT III

The Holder of Light
III

This power is the polar opposite to the Keeper of Time. The Holder of Light is the pattern to which light returns after the darkness of life and the density of manifestation. When the soul no longer belongs in the cycle of manifestation, it returns back into the light that is the spark of Divinity.

Please note that the use of the words 'darkness' and 'light' have nothing whatsoever to do with 'good' and 'bad'; rather they are pure expressions of Divine Power and its relation to substance.

This card tells us that something has become completely withdrawn from our inner and outer realms and has returned to the Divine Source. When this card appears in a magical reading, it tells us that something is complete in the Divine sense. It no longer has a function in the Physical world, the Underworld, or the Inner realm: it has rejoined its source. It is something laid to rest, something protected. It is the deepest Divine Sanctuary where the soul takes refuge.

Mundane Divination: Something returning to source after completion, going into hibernation, withdrawing in the deepest sense, completion, hiding one's light, remaining hidden and safe.

ARCHON & AION

The Archon and the Aion

The Archon and the Aion are the threshold-keepers of Divinity. The two powers are opposing beings, a bit like the positive and negative poles of a magnet. They are archangelic in their structure and stand between Divinity and the manifest outer and inner worlds.

Between them they create an energetic tension that forms a barrier through which nothing is allowed to pass unless it truly belongs there. The two archangelic beings are Divinity's guardians, its 'doormen.'

The Archon is the overseer who grants passage only to souls seeking a return to the Holder of Light. The Aion is the door-opener who lets through the flow of the Divine Spark as it seeks to express itself in the inner and outer worlds.

This card shows us the images of the two archangels. One holds a shield to protect; the other offers a cup. The cup dispenses the pattern of time/light into creation. The shield protects the threshold of Divinity. It also protects the magician from their actions by blocking them from stepping into the Divine realm.

The appearance of this card tells of a dangerous threshold that has been reached and which must not be crossed, for the power beyond this threshold is too great. While the power beyond this threshold is not destructive, its sheer might would threaten a mere mortal.

To ignore this card's warning is not to be punished, but to be potentially destroyed or irreparably damaged. It tells us that something beyond this threshold is too powerful for our consciousnesses or manifest bodies to cope with. If the barrier's force is tested by a magician, then they will be impacted by a defensive blow.

When this card appears in a magical reading, it indicates that the magician has reached a threshold which it is not yet safe to pass across. Its advice is to stop and wait.

Mundane Divination: There is a danger ahead, so wait. You are reaching the limit of something at this time, and a temporary barrier is there for your own good; wait and watch. The limit could be physical, mental, energetic, economic, or a limit of distance. Whatever you are doing a reading for, when this card turns up in a prominent or 'path ahead' position, the message is that you need to pause and rethink, or at least wait.

Chapter II

The Inner Realm: Abyss and Root Powers

Behind the veil of all the hieratic and mystical allegories of ancient doctrines, behind the darkness and strange ordeals of all initiations, under the seal of all sacred writings, in the ruins of Nineveh or Thebes, on the crumbling stones of old temples and on the blackened visage of the Assyrian or Egyptian sphinx, in the monstrous or marvelous paintings which interpret to the faithful of India the inspired pages of the Vedas, in the cryptic emblems of our old books on alchemy, in the ceremonies practised at reception by all secret societies, there are found indications of a doctrine which is everywhere the same and everywhere carefully concealed.

— Alphonse Louis Constant
(Eliphas Levi)

The Inner Realm is the universe's 'cooking pot,' and is where the various beings and forces reside that are involved in the creation and destruction of life and everything in the living world. It is also the realm where we find guardians and inner contacts, and all the constructions with which the mystical-magical human can connect, such as the Inner Library (Divine records), the inner temples, and so forth.

It may be pertinent to point out that the use of the word 'inner' does not mean it is inside your mind; it means that it has no physical expression. We use our minds in vision and dreams to connect with this place, but it is a realm that exists beyond the human mind, just as the Physical Realm exists beyond your body.

In these two chapters on the Inner Realm, we will examine, in descending order, its beings, powers, and places. We will start in this chapter with six of the ten *core root powers*. Three of these powers appear in the Divine Realm, and six in the Inner Realm. The tenth power is the beginning, and also the sum total, of the Physical Realm. This chapter also includes the Abyss as the highway of creation and destruction, and the being that is the bridge across the Abyss. The next chapter will introduce you to the many other powers and contacts that work in the creative process of life expression, many of whom work closely with humanity.

ABYSS

The Abyss

The Abyss is a highway of power and time that flows from 'above' to 'below.' New life forming falls down from the heights and meets the utterance/expression of the Divine as it crosses the level of the Abyss, which presents in the Inner Realm. At that meeting point stands the Keeper of the Abyss, a bridge between the Divine Realm and the Inner Realm, and here the newly forming life combines with the utterance/light of the Divine. From there it starts to travel across the Inner Realm into life expression in the Physical Realm.

The Abyss also flows down into the deepest depths of the Underworld, like a shaft that runs through all the worlds. It is this 'back room' shaft of time and power that separates the Divine Realm from all the other realms. The Divine Realm is timeless, ever-powerful, and ever-existing, whereas all the other realms, on the other side of the Abyss, are realms of creation and destruction, and thus mortal, with a limited span of time.

Although the Abyss is listed under the Inner Realm, its colour border is black for the Underworld. This is because, though a magician mainly accesses the Abyss in vision via the Inner Realm, working with it as a place at the *start* of creation, adepts also access the Abyss from the depths of the Underworld while working in service in the realm of *death*. The Abyss is at both the beginning and the end of formation/creation. We humans think in very simple dimensions, but the realms are vastly more complex than we can ever imagine.

The appearance of this card in a powerful reading can mark a major turning point in a magician's life path. It is a step from which there is no going back: a potentially dangerous step, but one that can move the magician forward in their deeper understanding of magic, power, Divinity, and life.

You can choose whether or not to move forward. Choosing not to will close that opportunity down; to choose to step forward is literally to step off the cliff and surrender to Divine Power. This dynamic, in its most magical form, is the visionary act known as 'crossing the Abyss.'

Although the adept candidate must undergo such visionary trials, it is a natural dynamic that plays itself out in the lives of individuals, societies, and also nature. The appearance of this card in a magical reading can indicate that the magician has reached a junction point in their lives where they must decide either to step into the deep unknown, putting their life in the hands of the Divine, or to step back, away from destruction.

The Abyss can also appear in a magical reading to show that openings have formed between the Underworld realm and the Physical realm, enabling destructive beings to surface. The Abyss reaches to the bottom layers of the Underworld, and is the long-term storage facility for all the realms. All beings with no purpose in manifestation sleep deep down in the Abyss in caves or in sealed-up places at the bottom of the Abyss. This card can appear in times of danger, disease, or when destructive forces are unleashed on the world.

Mundane Divination: A potential for destruction: something destructive can be released if you are not careful. In health readings it can depict pain and sickness that can get out of control. It is a card that tells of 'reaching rock bottom' before the dawn finally arrives. If it appears prominently in a reading or at its end, then it can be a warning: in such a case, use divination to look at alternative actions that would change the future path.

But when earth had covered this generation also—they are called blessed spirits of the underworld by men, and, though they are of second order, yet honor attends them also—Zeus the Father made a third generation of mortal men, a brazen race, sprung from ash-trees; and it was in no way equal to the silver age, but was terrible and strong. They loved the lamentable works of Ares and deeds of violence; they ate no bread, but were hard of heart like adamant, fearful men. Great was their strength and unconquerable the arms which grew from their shoulders on their strong limbs. Their armor was of bronze, and their houses of bronze, and of bronze were their implements: there was no black iron. These were destroyed by their own hands and passed to the dank house of chill Hades, and left no name: terrible though they were, black Death seized them, and they left the bright light of the sun.

— Hesiod, *Works and Days*

KEEPER OF THE ABYSS

The Keeper of the Abyss

The Keeper of the Abyss is an archangelic being sometimes described as Metatron. Although this power is angelic, it also has aspects of humanity within it. This being operates only as a bridge across and within the Abyss, and ensures that everything is in its place. It ensures that those who sleep down in the Abyss stay there, that those who must rise from the Abyss do so, and that those who should cross the Abyss are assisted.

The Keeper also facilitates the future life potentials that are flowing down from above and mediates it/them towards the manifest world. This is a deep and powerful being on the threshold of Divinity who acts as a crossroads.

The appearance of this card tells the magician that deep, formative powers are crossing a threshold towards manifestation, and that by meditating with this being in mind they can draw deep understanding of this process. It signifies a major crossroads and reminds us to choose wisely which direction we take. The appearance of the Keeper of the Abyss in a reading can also indicate that the magician is being protected for their own good or is being guided on matters of the Abyss. It can also indicate guardianship of the adept. The Keeper of Abyss, as a mediator or bridge, also takes some responsibility for that which crosses or passes through it. The actions of this being are bridging and mediating, but also holding, protecting, and guarding.

Mundane Divination: This card can appear in mundane divination when the subject of the reading is being protected from stepping forward at the wrong time, when their fate is being protected.

LIGHT BEARER IV

The Light Bearer
IV

The Light Bearer is an archangelic being who helps forge the path of the Divine Spark on its journey into life expression. It is the first of the ten core powers to express in the Inner Realm; the previous three make up the powers of the Divine Realm. It is a defined power that has an instinctive impulse to manifest into a vessel (life, body, the earth). It guides the light to substance, and it is also the light within the earth.

This being affects everything that comes near it; and as the Divine Spark flows from the pattern of Hidden Knowledge, it interacts with the Light Bearer, who creates and upholds a path for that passage into life. It is a positive power, a power that seeks life expression. It is the pure light which is in everything.

When this card appears, it tells of a pure essence of something, or of an original impulse. It tells of a new path being forged with Divine assistance, of the light within the darkness, the shine at the end of a long tunnel. It is a giving and merciful angelic power that can open the way for the magician to move forward, but it will not directly assist or interact with the magician. The Light Bearer builds the path into the future through which the fate pattern can express itself: it is the Opener of the Way.

Mundane Divination: Forging ahead with a new path. A new path is being prepared and energized. This card can also indicate a power or person who is a 'trailblazer,' or a new beginning coming into formation. It is also a power that guides the soul through the darkness in its search for light.

IMPRISONER V

The Imprisoner
V

This angelic power works in opposition to the Light Bearer. Whereas the Light Bearer forges a path to completion, the Imprisoner closes paths, withholds the light, and traps everything that needs trapping in its power.

This being has multiple actions in the inner and outer realms. It is essentially a power of restriction. When it opposes the Light Bearer, it slows the creative impulse to a lower velocity and a lower frequency so that the Divine Spark can begin to take form and solidify: it acts like a braking system. It is the other end of the deep inner 'scales' with the life impulse on one side and the impulse to withdraw on the other. Another key word for this power is 'Strength.' It is the Divine strength, the only strength that can withhold the flow of life/power/existence.

This is the power that withholds life, a power that traps beings who should no longer be in circulation. It holds them until it is time for them to be released; or until it is time for the being or soul to travel back into life, or deeper into the arms of the Protector of Souls, or into the depths of the Abyss.

This is a very important dynamic for magicians to understand. These inner dynamics are imprinted on everything that exists, and it is within the balance of these two powers that magic is born. This card is the negative/dark to the positive/light of its partner, the Light Bearer. When this card appears in a reading, it can suggest the need to withhold something or put it in hibernation; or it can appear when the power of withholding is active in your magical life for some reason. It can also indicate powerful magical bindings at work that may need dealing with or removing.

Mundane Divination: Restriction, holding back or being withheld, imprisonment, suppression, the removal of time. Something is stopped from happening.

PURE BALANCE VI

Pure Balance
VI

The Angel of Pure Balance is a deep reflection of the scales of balance. It is the fulcrum that runs through everything, the fulcrum of the scales of Ma'at, and the fulcrum between the Light Bearer and the Imprisoner. It is also an angelic presence that sits in the centre of the inner realm powers, with the patterns of knowledge behind it, the Imprisoner to one side, and the Light Bearer to the other. It faces the future: the birth of substance and the manifestation of the physical realm.

This angelic being does not interact directly with humanity; rather it sits in the centre of all the power as it flows into manifestation and ensures that the powers of creation and destruction are evenly matched. It is the being most identified with root deities, ancient deities who have not been subdivided.

When this card appears in a reading, it tells of pure balance or of the power of a root deity. Depending on the questions asked, it can suggest where in a magician's life and work there is need for deep magical balance in the powers with which they are working, or it can indicate that such balance in their work has been achieved. It can also indicate to a magician working with angelic or deity powers that the power with which they have connected is a deep, resonant power of complete balance.

This should warn the magician to tread carefully, as a misstep or misjudgment can upset such a powerful, yet delicate balance. If the magician is in the midst of a round of magical work or a project then the appearance of this card can indicate where the centre of balance is for the magic. If bad cards also appear in relation to this, then they may be part of the balancing process, so should not be feared.

The magical power expressed through this card can be seen in action in the Ancient Egyptian *Book of Gates*, in the Fifth Hour, Scene 33, in which the Noble One, or Justified Adept, stands before Osiris in the Underworld.[1] The Noble One demonstrates to Osiris that he or she is able to *become* the fulcrum of the scales by stepping into the scales and being measured *as* a fulcrum. As such, this card is deeply connected to the Keeper of Justice. ρ. 63

Mundane Divination: When this card appears in a mundane reading, it can indicate things coming into balance. It is a card of harmony and success; but the power of balance is often accompanied by heavy responsibilities. It falls to you to maintain this newly-found balance and nurture it.

---

[1]Michael Sheppard and Josephine McCarthy. *The Book of Gates: A Magical Translation.* With illustrations by Stuart Littlejohn. Quareia Publishing UK, 2017, pp.132–135.

Day by day, what you choose, what you think and what you do is who you become.

Everything flows and nothing abides, everything gives way and nothing stays fixed.

No man ever steps in the same river twice, for it's not the same river and he's not the same man.

— Heraclitus (535–475 B.C.)

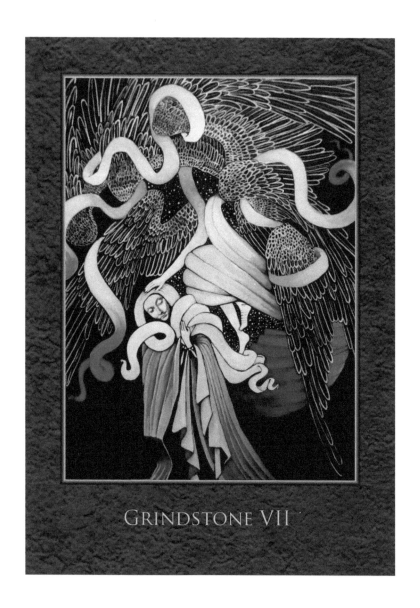

GRINDSTONE VII

The Grindstone
VII

Now we are getting to the inner powers that work more directly with humanity. The Grindstone is a lower octave of the Light Bearer and works closely with those humans willing to engage with its power. The Grindstone is an angelic being who creates boundaries and limitations which push a person to achieve. It is discipline and hard work that polishes the raw material into something very special. It is connected with the planetary power of Saturn. It is also the power behind the magical sword and self-limitation.

When the Grindstone appears in a reading, it tells of a period of intense work or potentially necessary hardship or necessary limitation. It is the power that holds the magician back so that they can perfect and learn new skills. It slows the magician's work and helps with the formation of the vessel or body's boundary, shape, and polish. It can also indicate the need for self-discipline.

The magical adept learns to work with the Grindstone and the Unraveller in equal measure to keep the scales balanced and to keep power flowing, but in a healthy, controlled, and mature way. This means that the magician must constantly pay attention not only to their magical work, but also to their health, their home, their resources, and how they conduct themselves in daily life.

Mundane Divination: A period of intense work, learning, or development. A hardship you cannot avoid, as it is developing you. Evolution through hard work; evolution through understanding that emotions should not govern you. Developing focus, power, strength, endurance. It can indicate a period of hardship, but it is something that you can cope with if you learn the lessons within the struggle.

UNRAVELLER

The Unraveller
VIII

We get to see this angelic power in action all around us in everyday life. It is the power that unravels us, tests us, and that can ultimately destroy us if we do not learn its lessons and maintain our awareness of its influence in our lives and in nature.

The Unraveller gives us rope—enough rope to hang ourselves. While the Grindstone stands over us and constantly teaches, limits, and polishes, the Unraveller stands back from the action and gives us everything we ask for to see whether we will destroy ourselves through self-indulgence or learn through such freedom to self-limit (which will bring the power of the Grindstone into our lives).

The Unraveller is power and substance unchecked. It can manifest as the literal overproduction of cells (cancer) where the self-limiting/death capacity of the cells has been disengaged; or it can manifest as too much wealth, too much substance (obesity, for example), overpopulation, lack of self-discipline or self-regulation, or the use of magic for unnecessary self-gratification or for settling everyday issues. All the manifestations of this angelic power bring destruction if we do not heed its warning and lessons.

When the Unraveller appears in a reading, it indicates that we are being given enough rope to hang ourselves, or that we are being given the opportunity to identify those parts of our lives or magical practice that are out of control. If we do not identify those areas—or choose not to—and we do not engage with the Grindstone, then we will seriously begin to walk the path to unravelling. A gentler, more positive expression of the Unraveller is the untangling or loosening of something to bring about balance. If something is tightly bound, trapped, overrestricted, or too tightly wound, then the Unraveller can unbind, loosen, and release it. However, once balance has been restored, if the power of the Unraveller is allowed to continue unchecked then it will undo all the good it has done by totally unravelling and destroying the focus of its attentions.

Mundane Divination: loss of discipline, loss of control, self-indulgence, greed, loosening of restrictions, unravelling a knotted situation, relaxing of tight restrictions, something in the early stages of decay and dissolution.

THRESHOLD GUARDIAN IX

Threshold Guardian
IX

The Threshold Guardian is a vast angelic being poised on the threshold of creation. It is the bridge between the inner worlds and the physical realm. This angel bridges life and consciousness back and forth between the Desert and the manifest world, allowing races, species, and individuals to flow into life.

The Threshold Guardian also guards the inner realms from human minds accidentally wandering into the inner worlds in dreams. It is this angel through which magicians pass when they seek entry to the inner worlds through the use of their imagination.

Its deeper power bridges the building blocks of life into the sea and land, bringing together the different ingredients that make up a physical form. It bridges the weave of the weaver into form to make a human, a dog, a tree, and so forth. It is an angel of alchemy in the deepest sense.

On another level, the Threshold Guardian triggers our imagination and dreams, giving us visions and enabling us to use our minds to cross deep into the inner worlds. It is the creative power in action, the regenerative pull of the moon, and the bridge of conception.

When this card appears in a reading, it heralds a period of creative, imaginative, and mental alchemy. It can also indicate a special pregnancy or a new, creative, living power about to flow into life. It is the bridge across which deep and ancient knowledge flows back into the world, the bridge that allows the vast powers of Divinity to flow into the land and enliven it.

Mundane Divination: This card represents a flow of energy, ideas, and creativity, and sometimes new life, new inspired experiences, and new works.

Note: The final card for the root powers, Mother Earth X, appears in the Physical Realm, as it represents the whole of the physical creation of our world and the completion of the combined powers of the Inner Realm.

Chapter III

The Inner Realm:
Other Powers and Contacts

Each one of us is part of the soul of the universe.

— Plotinus

PROTECTOR OF SOULS

The Protector of Souls

When souls have released from their bodies after death and begun their journey back through death, the Underworld, and the inner realms, one of the places they can end up is with the Protector of Souls. This female goddess power holds souls who need to sleep rather than be in life. She protects those who rest in the Underworld or the stars as they wait for the next stage of their development.

The message of this card is "wait." It signals a need to take time out, and to rest and regenerate before taking some final step, as another step forward would be unsafe. It is a compassionate barrier that holds us back until we are ready to move forward in whatever way is necessary.

We can also turn to this power if we are in the depths of complete depletion and exhaustion. Meditating upon her power and asking her for solace when we fear all is lost is one magical way to work with her. She is resonant with the goddess Isis, and she tends and protects those under her care.

Mundane Divination: A place of safety and shelter. This card tells of being shielded from events, of rest and regeneration, and the spirit seeking solace and quiet. This is the guardianship of the Mother who will tend to you when you truly need her care, offering you protection and solace.

WEAVER OF CREATION

The Weaver of Creation

The Weaver of Creation also sits close to the Abyss, opposite the Protector of Souls. The former creates patterns through which life/the soul can manifest, while the latter is the cloak that protects that which is exhausted, spent, and needs to rest. The Weaver of Creation gathers up the threads of light, energy, and power, and begins to form the physical world on her loom. She sets the pattern to which various angelic beings of the inner realm work in the formation of the worlds. This pattern then becomes the *Foundation of Knowledge* (see next card).

We cannot commune directly with the power of the Weaver as magicians, but her touch is in everything we see around us. The understanding of her pattern in every living thing helps us to understand the wider picture of creation and how everything is woven tightly together.

When this card appears in a reading, it tells of complex dynamics coming together in formation, and it can indicate the creator of something. The Weaver, whose power runs through every structure made to last, Appears when a person decides to create a massive project, have a child, or begin a long-lasting magical lodge.

Where the Weaver lands in a layout will tell you what sort of creation is coming into being, be it magical, physical, or personal. It can also indicate where a long-term pattern is being created which is as yet unseen. She is expressed through the power of the Egyptian Goddess Neith, and the Greek Goddess Ananke, the Weaver.

Mundane Divination: This card can represent the creative power, or laying the ground for a new creative project. In a health reading, this card can also show the potential for conception or indicate pregnancy. It is a card of creativity, new projects, and new paths in life being formed. Occasionally it can also literally indicate someone who weaves.

HIDDEN KNOWLEDGE

Hidden Knowledge

Hidden Knowledge is a vast, complex angelic structure that has been created by the Weaver of Creation and which acts as a filter for Divine consciousness to flow through.

As the Divine Spark passes across the Abyss on its journey to the physical world, it passes through the angelic structure of Hidden Knowledge. Here it transforms from pure light with intent into breath, light, utterance, and the impulse to manifest physically. It might be worth mentioning here that the use of the word 'light' in respect to all these inner powers does not mean 'good/happy'; rather this light is a pure power that seeks expression.

The complex patterns known in mysticism by names such as 'The Flower of Life' or The Metatron Cube' are weaves of angelic consciousness, energy, power, and light that make up this filter we call Hidden Knowledge.

Once the Divine consciousness has passed through this filter, it begins to take on unique forms that will eventually become vessels for life: a human, a tree, the sun, an ocean, and so forth.

Working the other way, a magician who pushes deeper and deeper into the inner worlds will eventually come to this pattern. If they can connect with it, then they will be filtered and refined by its influence in preparation for access to the deepest mysteries. This process can take a long time, sometimes a lifetime, and it opens the magician's mind and heart to the profound aspects of magical and mystical knowledge.

When this card appears, it heralds a deep mystical revelation which may unfold quietly or suddenly confront the magician. It shows the magician that deep knowledge and understanding of the Mysteries is within their potential.

Depending on the question, this card can also indicate the need for something to remain a mystery and not be delved into, but be accepted as something unknown. It often appears in a reading where a hidden element which cannot yet be understood has an active influence. You do not need to know what it is at this stage, only that it is there. In its deepest form, this card can represent the deep and profound knowledge of the Divine awakening in the heart of the seeker.

Mundane Divination: When this card appears in a mundane reading, it can indicate an unknown element that needs to be there but remains hidden. It can indicate something you are not seeing, or a need to trust, or that the true knowledge of something is hidden deep within you.

INNER TEMPLE

The Inner Temple

The Inner Temple is the first card which depicts a place in the inner realm with a human connection. The Inner Temple represents all inner temples, which are themselves inner reflections of all consecrated sacred temples that have ever existed in the physical realm. It also can represent 'The' Inner Temple that groups of adepts construct and work within as part of their stream of magic. It is the deepest, most balanced expression of Divine mystical magic that bridges between Divinity and Humanity.

The Inner Temple is where we meet deep inner contacts, inner adepts, the inner priesthoods, and the ancient deity powers. Magical adepts work in the inner temples as part of their magical work, connecting with angelic beings, deities, and contacts who once took part in human life.

The Inner Temple often appears in magical readings when there is a connection between the inner temples and the magician. Sometimes such a connection can be made years before the magician first becomes aware of it. The contacts of the inner temples wait until the magician is ready to recognize them and work with them.

Whenever and wherever this card appears in a magician's reading, it tells the magician that the powers and contacts of the inner temples are active in their work. It can also highlight the beginning of magical work with an ancient deity. Before such a deity becomes active with a magician, a threshold is prepared for the interaction. The inner temple power is part of that process. It is also a powerful indicator that the magician is moving away from everyday magic into deeper, more powerful, mystical magic.

Mundane Divination: There are deep inner dynamics at work even in a mundane situation. It can mean that inner voices of intuition are to be followed, that the person or situation is being guided by something greater than themselves. It signals that outer life events are being overseen by the gods, and that there is a hidden, deeper dynamic at work.

Mádimi

INNER LIBRARIAN

The Inner Librarian

The Inner Librarian is a major inner contact for many different types of magicians who resides exclusively in the Inner Library. The Inner Library is a more accessible aspect of the Inner Temple, and is usually the first place that apprentice and Initiate magicians work as they develop their inner skills.

The Inner Librarian is a consciousness that is both of humanity and also of a deity. This being is the keeper of human knowledge, and works exclusively for the attainment and protection of knowledge and wisdom through the ages.

When this card appears in a reading, it indicates that the magician would benefit greatly from working in the Inner Library, and is potentially being called to work in the Inner Library. It can also indicate a new phase of learning, one assisted by inner guidance if the magician pays attention. It is a card of intensive study and of learning from the experience of previous generations of magicians. It can also indicate a new teacher coming into the magician's life.

Mundane Divination: Someone of integrity who will guide and teach you. A new period of learning. Listen to your heart and instincts, as a power is guiding you. This card can also appear in mundane readings to indicate formal study, going back to school, or learning new skills.

INNER COMPANION

The Inner Companion

The Companion is an inner contact who works with mystics, visionaries, priests, and magicians who have been granted access to the inner realm of the Desert by the Desert Guardians. Most of the time, the Inner Companion is an angelic being, but on rare occasions it is a Justified Adept who is not living, who exists in the inner realms to guide and protect those who seek out the Mysteries.

The role of the Companion is to guide and advise the seeker as they begin to explore the inner worlds in the pursuit of learning and service. Usually this contact is made by working in magical vision to access the inner realms, though they sometimes appear spontaneously in dreams and visions.

In Kabbalah this Companion is known as *Sandalphon*, an angelic consciousness that also has human elements and which works alongside humans in the outer and inner worlds. This contact's role is to guide the seeker's actions, to help them understand the outer world's inner template, and to help the seeker understand how the two worlds are within and of each other.

This card indicates that the person or situation that is the reading's subject is part of a larger developmental process, and that inner guidance is there for the seeker: the Companion will be by their side.

This contact will not save you from yourself. Nor will it do things for you or show you things that you should find out for yourself. It guides you towards your own path, and reveals those parts of the Mysteries that you can currently understand. Like a true friend it does not do things for you, but helps enable you to learn, grow, and be useful.

Mundane Divination: you are not alone: a power greater than you is watching over you and guiding you.

GUARDIANS OF THE INNER DESERT

Guardians of the Inner Desert

This inner being guards the Mysteries. It blocks passage to the deeper inner worlds, and keeps the seeker from accessing inner powers that they are not able or ready to understand and respect. If the seeker tries to push past this guardian, then they will be catapulted out of the inner worlds or diverted down a blind alley. The guardian is there both to protect the integrity of the Inner Mysteries and to protect you from your own stupidity.

When you arrive at a point where it is safe for you to continue on your path, the wall will dissolve and the guardian will step aside to grant you access to the deeper realms. Never disregard the guardian: he is there for your protection and benefit. When we are young, we want things and we want them now. This being teaches us that 'want' means nothing. As we mature, we see the wisdom of restriction and the importance of working both within our capabilities and within the time of natural order.

In a reading, this card warns us to stop and think about what we are doing and why. It tells the reader there is potential danger ahead and they should tread slowly and cautiously. It can also indicate, depending on its position in a layout, that the magician is protected by inner guardians and that whatever destruction or danger is flowing around them will not penetrate them.

Mundane Divination: You have reached a limit, or your way ahead is being blocked for good reason, as what lies beyond the guardians is dangerous. When this card appears in a mundane reading, pay attention to what in your life is being blocked. Do not try to move beyond this block, as it is there for your own good. It is a security barrier, a protective wall.

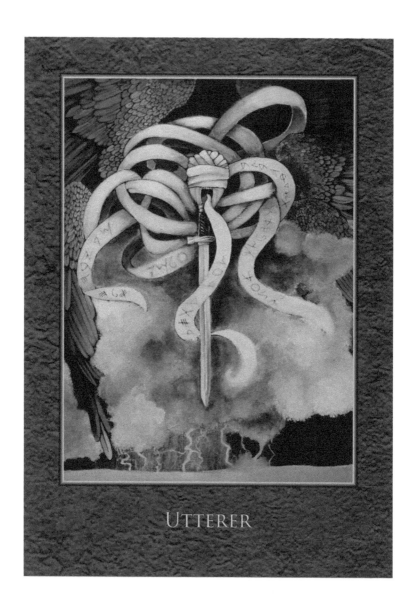

UTTERER

The Utterer

The Utterer is the mediator of the power of utterance. It is also the angelic being who whispers the words of God into the ears of humanity. When the Divine Breath is to be spoken upon earth, the Utterer whispers in the ears of those who can hear.

This angel is the threshold of mediation between humanity and Divinity through the breath, through sound. It is the power that breathes the Divine Spark into a form that becomes life. It is also the power that gifts humanity with sacred sound, alphabets, and the knowledge of God.

When this card appears in a reading, the message is "pay attention." Something is being uttered into the world that directly affects you. Just pay attention, listen, learn, and let the angel breathe and utter through you, whether that means uttering poetry, wisdom, sacred words, or a storm. The Utterer in its natural form on the earth expresses *a wind that brings change*. It is the power behind sacred utterance, sacred song, and the voices of humans who utter to the Divine. The Utterer not only carries messages from the Divine to humanity, it also carries the words of humans to Divinity and the Gods.

The Utterer can also carry messages: when it appears in a reading, it could be telling you that an important message is coming. The message may be as subtle as a whisper, but it will be of great power in your life. It could also be a reminder for you to guard your words, so think carefully about what you are saying, writing, or teaching. Words have power, and words spoken by a magician have a great deal more.

Mundane Divination: Important news or information is coming; or it can indicate 'important speech' such as teaching, lecturing, or writing, or otherwise conveying information that is important.

KEEPER OF JUSTICE

Keeper of Justice

The Keeper of Justice is probably one of the best-known images in the Western world. The Keeper of Justice is an angel blindfolded. This shows us that its power is indiscriminate: it cannot be swayed by emotion, as it cannot see. It holds the sacred sword ready for action, and the scales—and as you can see, the angel *is* the scales, unlike the deity of Justice, who *holds* the scales.

The angel is the fulcrum that upholds the scales, and as such represents the highest form of Ma'at. Becoming the fulcrum is one of the high achievements in adept magic: you are neither good nor bad, you simply uphold balance. Upholding balance and restoring balance is one of the main jobs of a Justified adept. This ability is tested in the Underworld at one's initiation, and again in one's death passage through the Underworld. The spirit of a dead adept stands before the deity in the Underworld and demonstrates their ability to become the fulcrum of the scales of Ma'at, the scales of true Justice.

Divine justice has nothing to do with right and wrong in a moral sense: it is about cause and effect. When this card appears in a reading, it tells of an action of Justice—a rebalancing of the scales or a period of balance—either unfolding in the subject's life or being on its way. It is impossible to uphold balance all the time and still live, but striving towards upholding balance in everything you do allows the Gates of the Mysteries to open before you.

Mundane Divination: In a mundane reading, the appearance of this card can mean balance, the restoration of equilibrium, or literally Justice. It can represent the law, law courts, or the dispensing of Justice.

CHARIOT

Chariot

The Chariot card has various connotations from the magically mundane to the deeply mystical. On a mundane level, this card indicates travel, inner or outer. But the Chariot is also much more than this.

The Chariot is made up of archangelic beings that lift the human to the threshold of Divinity—the closest a human can come to Divinity and still live. In the life of a magician there comes a time when such contact is possible, and it often occurs without warning. It can happen while working in vision or while deep in dreams.

This angelic power, the Chariot, is deeply connected with the power of Metatron, the angel that stands at the junction between Divinity in its most powerful form, and humanity.

This card can indicate that the magician is about to step into a powerful arena where the archangelic powers, Divine consciousness, and magical humanity all come together in mystical union. The magician is lifted briefly by the Divine vehicle of the Chariot to inner paradise and looks upon the power of the Divine realm.

It is the Barque of Re that carries the solar deity through the stars and the Underworld, and the Chariot within which the adept 'rides' as they reach to become one with the stars. The Wheels of Fate, angelic beings connected with the land, drive the Chariot out of the land and up into the stars. The Chariot is of the inner realm, but it rises out of the physical land. It is closely connected with the mystical Mysteries of *ascension*.

Mundane Divination: In a mundane reading, the Chariot can appear when one will go on an important journey, as the Chariot is connected to the Wheel of Fate. It can also literally indicate a 'car' or mode of transport.

WHEEL OF FATE

Wheel of Fate

As the Wheel of Fate turns, it burns up old, outmoded patterns and illumines the new path ahead. This power sits close to humanity and manifestation, and is involved with the changing tides of fate of all living things. (It is often mistaken for the Seraphim, which is a deeper, more powerful angelic being.) As the power of change flows through the Inner Desert, the Wheel turns and gives that change the momentum necessary to break the present stasis and prepare for whatever new allocations are to be put in place by the Three Fates.

The Wheel of Fate is connected to the Chariot: they are both powers that rise out of the earth and bring change. The Wheel is concerned with the fate patterns of living humans: it brings change that enables a person's fate to progress.

The appearance of this card heralds a major change for the magician or for the reading's subject. The area of the person's life which will manifest this change is indicated by where in the layout this card falls. It can also be read in conjunction with the Fates, should one of them appear in the same reading.

When this card appears, do not fear the change or fight it: it is a necessary part of your development and maturation. Embrace the change, and be open to engaging actively with this power to learn and grow.

Mundane Divination: Change is coming. The Wheel heralds change, for good or bad. Whatever the Wheel brings will enable a new path to be trodden, a new phase in one's life to unfold.

FATE GIVER

Fate Giver

The Fate Giver is one of the three goddesses who oversee and govern the fate of every living thing. The Fate Giver fixes the exact time and place of one's conception and birth, weaving into being all the gifts, potential developments, and fateful events of a life. She is the opener, the goddess who sets in motion the path of a new life. She takes the weave of creation that has passed over the threshold into physical form and turns it into a unique individual pattern.

The Fate Giver sets not only new lives in motion, but also new nations, religions, and patterns that are to express Divine potential in the manifest world. She fixes not only the conceptions and births of humans, but also those of other key living beings such as animals whose birth heralds a new epoch. She works in harmony with the stars and the Divine Inner Powers to manifest fully the weave created deep in the inner worlds.

For magicians, she is a key power to work with if one wishes to understand how the potential of life physically manifests through a fate pattern, and she also reveals what one's life will carry with it. We are all given pots of resources—gifts from the gods—when we are born. It is up to us to use these gifts wisely, and to learn to use them in the service of the land, humanity, and Divinity.

When this card appears in a reading, it shows that a starting point has been set in time, and a fate pattern is now actively in place within which a person or process can operate. Something has been set in motion, and is working to a specific pattern. This card can also indicate, depending on where it falls, the original potential or purpose of the reading's subject. It indicates the start of a new cycle, a new beginning, or a new life.

Mundane Divination: A new cycle begins, be it a new path in life or a major change that has been triggered. New directions, a major new phase of life.

FATE HOLDER

Fate Holder

The Fate Holder is also known as the Measurer: She Who Measures That Which Must Be Contained. She takes the Power of Restriction and applies it practically to every living thing.

This goddess sets a person's lifespan. Though there are many possible 'death hotspots' in a person's life—potential deaths that can be averted—no one can live beyond the measure of the Measurer.

We can call on her in times of danger and work with her magically to avoid potentially lethal dangers, so long as we are not at the end of our measure. Her measurements are of fate only, and are very specific: her whole focus is the timing of fate events, ensuring that all the threads of fate, along with our individual choices and actions, come together harmoniously.

Our futures are not set in stone; rather they are a complex pattern, a weave we can explore and travel down in our journey through life. Our individual actions and choices affect how we interact with that weave of fate. The Fate Holder ensures that we do not move beyond our own fate pattern, that we are contained within it; but how we experience that wider fate depends on our own actions and choices.

When this card appears, it tells us where fate is being measured and held, of a period of time within which something should be tackled. It can also indicate that a lifespan is being protected, or that a period of work or learning is still in progress and has not yet reached completion. It is a card of continuation, and the protection of that continuation.

Mundane Divination: a cycle is in progress, things are being held in place, all is well.

FATE TAKER

Fate Taker

The Fate Taker is the goddess power of completion: she cuts the thread of fate. She is the ending of something: a life, a way of life, a cycle of fate, and so forth. Once the end of the measure comes, the Fate Taker triggers the deeper inner powers that dismantle and compost something, or someone, with no future in the manifest world.

When she touches the web of fate, it dissolves and is no more. This can mean a literal time of death, or the end of something that will not come back. Whatever it is, it no longer has a pattern of fate through which it can manifest.

The position in which this card appears is very important to the reading's overall interpretation. If it falls in one of the inner positions or in the distant future, then it means that an ending has been set in time, but it has not yet manifested. If it appears in a physical realm position, then its position reveals where the ending expresses itself.

This card's appearance can indicate the end of a life, organization, cycle of fate, or activity that will not be revisited.

Mundane Divination: The end of something, completion, clearing the way for something new.

Chapter IV

The Physical Realm: Physical Structures and Natural Features

God has arranged all things in the world in consideration of everything else.

— Hildegard von Bingen

The powers of the Physical Realm are simpler for us to understand than those of the inner realm because they are around us all the time and are part of us. These powers flow through our world and manifest as powers, places, energy dynamics, and people. The powers of the inner realm flow through these outer expressions and directly affect us.

In a reading we can often see inner realm cards as the root causes of a situation and physical realm cards as their manifestation. Physical Realm cards are the commonest sort of card in the *Magician's Deck*, which is unsurprising considering the great diversity present in the manifest world.

In this chapter, *Physical Structures and Natural Features*, we will examine the group of cards that reflect structures built by humans, and natural features that are particularly important in divination. Some of these cards may not appear to be structures at first glance: Challenge of the Gods and Resources, for instance, look more like dynamics. But if you look more closely and meditate on their meanings, then you will see that they too are constructs that flow directly from humanity and magical construction.

MOTHER EARTH X

Mother Earth
X

Mother Earth is the land, the externalized expression of Divinity in substance and the true vessel of creation. The land is the container of the Divine Spark, just as our bodies are containers of the Divine Spark: everything manifest is Divinity exteriorized. The Mother Earth card tells us of the land, either the country where we live or the land or area where we live.

When this card appears in a layout, it is telling you of a land, a natural place, and of your relationship with it. Part of the work of a magical adept is maintaining an ongoing communion with the land and tending to its needs, a communion supported by attending to those messages from the land that appear in vision, synchronicities, and divination (like a card reading).

This card can also indicate that your magic needs more involvement from nature, or that the land is asking for help.

When you are asking a direct question, this card can often appear as an "it is all okay" card: Mother Earth is as she should be, and there is a balance of body and spirit. It can often be a "yes" card, or a completion card: Mother Earth is also the *Kingdom*, Malkuth in Kabbalah, the final exteriorization of the Divine consciousness as it flows towards manifestation. This card says "job done." Something has been brought to completion, something that is just as it should be.

Mundane Divination: This is a success card, a completion card. It can also indicate a literal land. How you read it depends on the question: if you were reading about moving house and you wanted to look at a prospective place, then the appearance of this card would indicate that you have found the right place for you.

SOL

Sol

The sun is the source of our life. Without it we cannot survive, and nothing grows. The elemental power that flows to us from the sun is powerful and raw, and it can be worked with magically in a variety of ways. The sun's magical consciousness is vast, and a primal deity power flows from it with no human filters or dressings: it is just pure power.

In the modern rush for glamour in magic, the sun's power is often overlooked, but that was not always the case. Our ancestors and ancient priesthoods knew full well the power that flows from the sun—not merely sunlight's mundane ability to promote health, growth, and regeneration, but also the magical inner power that flows from the sun. When Sol appears in a reading, it can indicate great success or access to a vast reserve of power, depending on the question and where the card falls.

In health readings the card can indicate burning—too much fire power concentrated in one area—depending on the question and the position in which it falls.

The power of the sun is vast and not to be underestimated: it can burn, it can destroy, it can spit radiation. If you look closely at the myths concerning Re, the Egyptian sun god, then you will get a much better picture of the range of powers represented by this card.

Mundane Divination: Success, energy, heat, and evolution. Where this card falls, it brings with it tales of victory, large reserves of energy, and visible success.

LUNA

Luna

The magical power of the moon lives up to its magical persona: a power difficult to grasp, whose hidden depths threaten to drown those who delve too deeply into its mysteries. The moon's magical power governs psychic inner sight, the tides of the sea, the pull of fertility, and the rhythms of nature. More superficially, the moon is a power of night, shades, shadows, fertility, and the pull of reproduction. The power of the Moon can be used to hide things, to slip unseen into places, to draw on sexual powers, and to be lost in the shadows of moonlight. It is the silver of the magical path: the humans are of 'silver', and the Gods are of 'gold'.

On a deeper magical level, the moon's power helps us understand the gifts and powers which run through ancestral bloodlines: it is a lower octave of the Threshold Guardian IX. When this card appears, we are confronted with the complexity that is Luna. Its meaning is like its nature: whenever we seek to grasp its wisdom, it slips through our fingers. It is a changeable power like the tides, and should be understood in such terms.

Read this card in relation to everything around it, and according to where it falls in the layout. Rather than telling you something specific, Luna casts a shadow of confusion, depth, and illusion on its fellow cards in a reading. It tells you that you are not seeing the whole story, that something may be masked or veiled, or that strange and disturbing tides could be affecting the situation.

This card can also indicate the loss of sanity, and warns the magician against pushing their mind and imagination too far. It can tell of timings and tides of magic, and brings to the reading a quality of unpredictability and inspiration.

Mundane Divination: In a mundane reading this card can indicate that you are not seeing the full picture, that there is a hidden element, or that something that has not yet developed enough for you to see it clearly. It can indicate foggy thinking, being overly dramatic, being lied to, and being untruthful with yourself.

PLACE OF HEALING

Place of Healing

This is the water that soothes and heals, the water that refreshes and regenerates. It is the natural cold spring that rises from the land and nourishes everything in its path. It is the domain of healing spirits, of compassionate goddesses, and the vital force of life that flows through the water.

When this card appears, it can indicate a diseased body healing, a period of rest and regeneration after hard work, or the path towards balance. This card tells us of a withdrawal from the hectic world of power and indicates a place and space to heal and regenerate. It is a sanctuary of regeneration, and the literal healing of body, mind, and soul.

If the reading is about a land area or place, then it can literally mean that a healing spring is on the land and should be worked with. In the reading of an individual it indicates a period of regeneration. If it appears in a reading about magical work, then it can indicate the power of healing and regeneration, or the necessity of working with water in some healing capacity.

Mundane Divination: When this card appears in a mundane reading, it can indicate a mental or physical healing process, or simply that the worst is over. The subject of the reading is in a 'healing place' either literally or figuratively.

INSPIRATION

Inspiration

The Waterfall is the dynamic flow of inspiration, creative expression, and inner voices into the manifest world. Water is a powerful substance not only for the obvious, mundane reasons, but also for its ability to carry energetic information and spread it across the land.

It is important for magicians to utilize this power, and it is of the utmost importance for all magical people to engage consciously with it. What is simply a creative inspiration in an artist becomes a doorway into the inner realms for a magician.

In this card, the waterfall is upheld by two angelic beings who help mediate the deeper powers of imagination, which in turn mediates access to the Inner Realms. The magician creates through inspiration, then steps through their imagination into non-physical realms.

When this card appears, it shows that a creative, inspirational force is present or coming, a force that can be mediated magically through art, music, poetry, stories, sculpture, etc. It indicates a creative impulse that comes from a much deeper well than the reader's own mind. A voice or voices from deep within the inner worlds are whispering an inspiration that could lead the magician down the path of mediating something new to the world.

It can also represent what *The Book of Gates* calls "cold refreshment," the inner power of water that extinguishes a destructive fire.[2] This cooling refreshment is the product of a magician's own balance and harmony. It is a very good card, and when it appears in a magical reading it can point to energies that are cooling, regenerative, and that bring evolution to the soul.

Mundane Divination: This card is one of coolness, water, inspiration, creativity, and a move towards health. In a health reading it is the flow of fluids in the body that heal and regenerate. It is the life-giving water, the holy water, and the flow of energy that is productive, healthy, and creative.

---

[2]Sheppard and McCarthy, *The Book of Gates: A Magical Translation*, p.33.

TEMPLE OF ANCESTORS

Temple of Ancestors

A circle of sharp, upright stones forms an ancestral alignment which is dwarfed by the vast body of water that tumbles past it. In the same way, we are small and insignificant in the face of the forces of nature. The river of ancestors falls powerfully past the stones, just as the consciousnesses of our ancestors and the bloodlines of our lands flow constantly around us.

This card represents the collective knowledge of all who have gone before us. For magicians, the place it represents is a focal point for learning from the past experiences of others. It is an outer version of the Inner Library, and allows us to tap into the vast reservoir of ancestral wisdom that connects us to the land and the powers that flow through it.

When this card appears, it is telling us that there is access to ancestral wisdom in a place or situation, and we can choose to engage with it. Where the card appears in the layout tells us where in our magical lives this resource is active and accessible. If it appears in the position of Home and Hearth, for example, then the wisdom and knowledge we seek can be found in our own family line, land, or community.

This card can also indicate that an ancestor is trying to teach us or assist us in some way. Such ancestral guidance or teaching can be good or a hindrance: ancestral structures and collectives often do not think in the same ways as modern people, and the Ancestral Temple can sometimes be a difficult contact to work with as its aims and objectives can be very different to modern ideas.

Mundane Divination: In a mundane reading this card can point to traditional skills, old ways and wisdoms, and family ancestors keeping an eye on you and trying to help. It can also represent a very old or ancient organization whose outer expression has faded in the minds of most people, but is still active nevertheless.

MAGICAL TEMPLE

Magical Temple

When the Magical Temple card appears, it tells us about magical structure. The Magical Temple card represents the outer court structure of magic: training, practice, or a magical community.

The Magical Temple is about form and structure. It is the building, the grades, the outfits, the tools... the complete exteriorization of magic in the magician's life. Now this can be a good thing or a bad thing. Some structure and form is good, as it contains magic, gives it shape, and ensures the long-term survival of the style, content, or path.

A true Magical Temple must keep a precarious balance between form and flow, between identity and anonymity: a healthy Magical Temple will have all that is necessary for the magic to flow and nothing that can limit, strangle, or degenerate it.

Like all cards, when this card appears in a reading, it must be read in the context of the question and its position. In a good position, it tells of a magical structure that is enabling magic to flow through your life. It can also represent magical training or a magical community around you that helps you flourish as a magician.

If it lands in a difficult position, then it may mean that the magician is clinging to outdated forms and unnecessary dressing: the structure is limiting your development and needs to be let go. It is easy to get trapped in a beautiful or interesting cage, and the trap of a glamorous temple is large indeed.

If the question can possibly relate to inner visionary magic, then it could also represent the inner structure of the magical temple, the one for that specific magical system and its patterns. Where it lands and what the question is dictate how this card should be understood.

Mundane Divination: In a mundane reading, this card can represent an organization with skills that affect the person doing the reading. For example, it can represent a hospital where skills are used in a specific way, or a government organization that has an effect or influence on the reader. It is a card of organized structure and skill, like a university, government, medical organization, and so forth.

RIVER OF DREAMS

River of Dreams

There are many types and qualities of sleep, but for a magician the realm of dreams can be very important. Sometimes dreams are just, well, dreams. Other times, the dream state becomes an in-between place where we work, interact, or are given glimpses into what is around us and what is to come.

The magical dream state is represented in the card River of Dreams. The River of Dreams itself is an inner flow of energy that we perceive as a river flowing from the Underworld—from the same source as the River of Death. It carries with it ancient memories, and also acts as a source of energetic communion between faerie beings, ancestors, the newly dead, the inner contacts, and humans.

When we dream, our conscious control over how we interact and 'see' falls into the shadows and our deeper selves, instincts, and true reactions surface. Because the annoying barrier of our conscious mind is relaxed, inner contacts can sometimes connect more easily, and our capability for necessary inner sight becomes stronger.

When this card appears in a magical reading, it could indicate that you are working magically in your sleep, or that you need to allow your body extra sleep time for some necessary contact, work, or prophetic sight.

It can also indicate a need for visionary work, or even for literally walking in the rivers of the Underworld in your work.

Mundane Divination: This card represents the dream state, sleep, meditations, and deep creative expression. If it appears in a reading, then depending on the question and context it may indicate a need to spend more time sleeping, or that you should keep a dream diary to spot the messages your deeper self is trying to tell you.

GATE OF THE PAST

Gate of the Past

This card signifies the past that we have left behind. If it appears in a reading, then it shows that something is either now in the past, or that something from the past is affecting the present or future. This card is a doorway rather than a being or person, and tells us of things left behind.

If this card falls in a difficult position, then it can indicate that we may be trying to hang on to the past or that we are looking backwards: it is a warning that we need to move on and strike a path that moves forwards, not backwards.

It can also, for magicians, indicate the need to work in the Underworld, as the gate is also indicative of the gates of the Underworld.

Mundane Divination: Something is moving into the past, or something from the past is having an effect on the present and potential future. If this card appears in a position which may be difficult, then it can be a clue that the resolution to the problem lies with the past: either bringing something to a conclusion, or letting the past go.

HOME & HEARTH

Home and Hearth

This card is probably one of the simplest in the deck. It represents the home, family, and domesticity. This card tells us of our domestic responsibilities, our home life, our family, and our 'tribe.' It can also warn us about becoming too comfortable, about relaxing and not forging ever forward in the quest of learning and service.

On a deeper level, Home and Hearth is a stage of magical initiation where the seeker is lulled into the cosy security of the family. Either we succumb to the comfort and security of the Home and Hearth and push no further on our quest for the Divine, or we peer through the window to see the temple beyond on the horizon—the ever-present reminder that a mystical or magical seeker can never truly retire. We can rest, recoup, and regenerate, but we can never really stay. The path of the seeker is always calling, and answering the call means leaving the warmth and tenderness of the hearth and forging ever onward.

When this card appears in a magical reading, it can mean a period of rest and relaxation, or it can indicate the group, tribe, or community that the magician feels is his or her family.

Mundane Divination: This is the card of home and family, and will appear when such a thing is important in your life at that time. It can also, depending on layout and position, indicate that something important is connected with your home or family. It can be literally your house, your family, or where you feel most at home. It can also point to more time being spent at home on mundane things, rest, and recuperation.

PATH OF HERCULES

Path of Hercules

The Path of Hercules is the path that leads to the short-term future: it is the way ahead. It is called the Path of Hercules as it is also a magical path, the path that forges the magician as he or she strides into the future: it is a Herculean task to walk such a path with all its trials and challenges.

Magically, the path vanishes off into the magical direction of south, the direction of potential and formation. When this card appears in a reading, it is telling you about the way ahead. It is read in conjunction with the position in which it lands, and can indicate the best way forward for a course of action or decision; or it can indicate that a new path has appeared for the magician, a path that will lead to new cycles of fate. It is a card full of new potential and new opportunities, and is the path that leads to magical adepthood.

Mundane Divination: The Path of Hercules shows in mundane readings when a new path is opening up, or when a path ahead has been cleared, ready for the person to walk it. It shows new potentials, and literally the way ahead. It is a positive card, and can show the light at the end of the tunnel for people who have been struggling.

CHALLENGE OF THE GODS

Challenge of the Gods

This is a bit of a 'wild card,' and tells of a fate path being manipulated directly by the deities and beings who operate within the human patterns of fate. It turns up in readings when something much bigger is going on, something which will often remain unseen by those involved in the fate pattern.

When this card appears in a reading, it can indicate a struggle for achievement and trials a magician must undergo to grow. It is a positive but tough card: it is the sort of situation where the magician is having to deal with difficult work or life events in order for them to learn and grow stronger. The card is heavily involved in fate, and in the magical connections between the inner worlds, the deities, and the magician.

It is the chessboard where the deities move the magician into places and situations where whatever is necessary can happen. No matter how difficult the situation, knowing that it is a stepping stone on a fate path can help one forge forward. The secret of this card is that no matter how tough the struggle, it is fated, and the magician will not face it alone, for the gods are watching over them.

Mundane Divination: In mundane readings this card can mean that adversity lies ahead, but it promises a good conclusion. It is the struggle before success, the light before the dawn. It is the challenge of life that strengthens you. If the card appears in a health reading, then the person needs a close eye keeping on them: some struggles are worth it, and some are not. If this card appears and other options look worse, then the path indicated by this card will be a struggle, but ultimately successful.

INNER SANCTUM

Inner Sanctum

The Inner Sanctum is the vessel which holds the pure spark of Divinity. It is a place that is sacred—truly sacred—and which mediates the power of Divinity to humanity and the world at large. For us, this usually manifests as a temple, a church, and so forth. It tells of a place where the presence of the Divine is strong, where we can bathe in the light and power of Divinity regardless of the specific religion or beliefs connected with the place. It can also indicate the Divine place 'within' – turning inwards to stillness and silence.

When this card appears in a reading it tells of such a sacred place, or of the need to go to such a place for safe haven or connection and communion with Divine Being. This card can be particularly helpful to a magician trying to find out about an ancient site or land area.

If this card appears in a reading for a person rather than a place, then it can indicate the need for the person to withdraw and meditate in a sacred place. Such places, regardless of the culture or religion to which they are connected, can give sanctuary, time out, strength, and peace to an overworked magician. They can also help plug the magician into the deeper, more mystical aspects of magic.

It can also indicate the stillness within someone, or that Divine protection has placed you in a more isolated situation. It is the presence of the Divine within, the sanctuary within which you are protected, and the sacredness around you.

Mundane Divination: If this card appears in a mundane reading, it may indicate a need to turn within and be still, a need to take time out and rest, or a special safe place.

RESOURCES

Resources

This card reflects the magical dynamics of personal inner and outer resources. Our health, vital force, wealth, inner sight, fertility, and so forth are all limited resources within our fate pattern. Everyone has their own individual measures according to what they need to achieve in their lifetime.

When this card appears in a reading, it tells of where a person's resources are being used most, so that the magician can preserve those resources to the best of their ability.

If this card appears in a difficult position, like the Gate of the Past or an Underworld position, then it can indicate that certain resources have been used up for a particular cycle, or that your resources are working deep in the Underworld for a while, and care must now be taken.

If new resources are coming in, then this card will appear in a future position. It can show when resources are being offered to you, or that resources are available for what you wish to achieve. Similarly, if the card shows in a withheld position, then this can be warning to tread carefully, as you are not fully resourced for what you are currently trying to achieve.

Mundane Divination: Depending on the position of the card, it can indicate that money, food, energy, or some other kind of help is available for you to achieve something. If it is in a withheld position, then it is warning you that your resources are low or less available than you may currently think, and that caution is advised.

Chapter V

The Physical Realm: Beings and Powers

Truly it has been said that there is nothing new under the sun, for knowledge is revealed and is submerged again, even as a nation rises and falls. Here is a system, tested throughout the ages, but lost again and again by ignorance or prejudice, in the same way that great nations have risen and fallen and been lost to history beneath the desert sands and in the ocean depths.

— Paracelsus

This short chapter outlines some of the inner powers of the land that can express in the physical realm and affect people, whether directly or indirectly. They are powers that can inhabit houses and harass or help the magician. They have their own chapter, as these powers can be strong, and they can have quite a marked effect on the life of the magician in one way or another. These are distinct powers and beings that reside in the land, and should you trigger them then you will have a better chance of interacting with them safely if you have a good understanding of their nature.

The cards can also indicate humans who possess their qualities, or who mediate, intentionally or otherwise, the personalities of these powers. This is often the case with mundane readings, or readings where people with specific, strong personalities are involved.

SPIRIT GUIDE

Spirit Guide

This card tells us about a powerful and ancient inner contact or 'spirit being' who works with visionaries, shamans, magicians, and mystics. It is a companion that appears as a white horse that flows out of the land, and which accompanies, guides, and protects humans as they begin to explore the inner worlds, the faerie realm, and the land's inner landscape.

Until a person can flow freely by themselves from one world or realm to another, the white horse acts as a guide, sometimes carrying the person on their backs as the magician learns how to access and explore places they did not know existed.

The more your work has to do with earth and nature, the more this companion will appear, until you have learned where things are and how to access them for yourself.

Many myths, from all over the world, tell of a magical white horse, often connected with the sun or the 'other world,' that assists kings, queens, visionaries, and magicians. This card does not always represent the 'White Horse': it can simply indicate a spirit willing to work with you as an inner contact, guide, or guardian, or even that you are about to start a new round of magical learning in a different realm of the inner worlds.

Mundane Divination: This card, in a mundane reading, shows when a guide or guardian is active in the life of someone or in a place. It can represent advice given in dreams, or a recently dead friend or family member who is keeping an eye on you to help you. Or it can indicate that a nature spirit is watching over you.

GOBLIN QUEEN

Goblin Queen

The power of the Goblin Queen was in the world before humans existed, and it will be still be here after humankind has gone. Her image represents tribal faerie beings or established lines of land beings rather than a literal contact. Her power is about the consolidation of territory, generations of control, and total confidence in the stability of her power.

When this card makes an appearance in a reading, it represents a magical connection with lines of Faerie or land beings who are firmly established within the land.

It is important to understand that when this card appears, it has nothing to do with whimsical, romantic, or New Age ideas of faeries. This card tells of us of the very real power these pre-human beings possess, and warns us that we have stumbled across an ancient base of faerie or land power that is well established and will be vigorously defended if necessary.

The Goblin Queen is fearless, powerful, and not above toying with a human for her own amusement. This deep and conscious power of the land is interested only in the continuance of its power and territory. Threaten either of those, and you will find yourself up against an enemy far beyond your capability. Pay homage to her power and offer service to the land as a magician, and you may just find yourself on the periphery of a vast, ancient, and protective family.

If the Goblin Queen makes an appearance in a magical reading, then it indicates a powerful faerie or land contact that is involved in, affected by, or at least aware of the situation being read about. The magician can then decide if they wish to make direct contact with that land power and work with them. If this card appears in an aggressive or dangerous reading, then it is very possible that the magician's actions have caused great offence or disturbance to the faerie lines this card represents. In such a case, the magician would be well advised to find a way to make amends as quickly as possible.

These beings are not cute, they are not reasonable, and they are not harmless. Land beings and faerie beings can devastate a person's life, home, family, and work should they choose to. They are most often found around areas with natural springs or stone outcrops. When the Goblin Queen's card appears, think very carefully about your magical actions and what effect they could have had on the land around you.

This card can also occasionally represent that type of female power that is beyond human confines, and can indicate an ancient female deity power with the same traits as the Goblin Queen. It can also represent such qualities running through a human woman who, often without her knowledge, has a deep and ancient blood or spirit connection with the faerie beings, a woman with deep reserves of power that she can tap. Such women can be feral as a result of that power until they learn to tame and focus it.

Mundane Divination: A woman who is more powerful than she appears, who is complex, skilled, and not above destroying someone or something to protect what she holds precious. This card represents a woman who is often not beholden to social or cultural norms and who will often confuse or confront people, but who is always true to the rule of nature. She is a human embodiment of nature in full tooth and claw.

Then it was that the Morrigan, daughter of Ernmas, came from the fairy dwellings, in the guise of an old hag, engaged in milking a tawny, three-teated milch cow. And for this reason she came in this fashion, that she might have redress from Cuchulain. For none whom Cuchulain ever wounded recovered without himself aided in the healing.

Cuchulain, maddened with thirst, begged her for a milking. She gave him a milking of one of the teats. "May this be a cure in time for me, old crone," said Cuchulain, and one of the queen's eyes became whole thereby.

He begged the milking of another teat. She milked the cow's second teat and gave it to him and he said, "May she straightway be sound that gave it." Her head was healed so that it was whole.

He begged a third drink of the hag. She gave him the milking of the teat. "A blessing on thee of gods and of non-gods, O woman!" And her leg was then made whole.

Now these were their gods, the mighty folk: and these were their non-gods, the folk of husbandry. And the queen was healed forthwith.

— *Táin Bó Cúalnge*
(*The Cattle Raid of Cooley*, from the Ulster Cycle)

FAERIE KING

Faerie King

The Faerie King is the counterpart of the Goblin Queen, but whereas she is a powerful defender of territory, the Faerie King is more of a trickster. This is the male aspect of faerie consciousness, and this card represents the type of being who will play havoc with a human settlement or individual not due to any territorial dispute, but purely for their own entertainment.

Like the beings represented by the Goblin Queen, these faerie beings do not have human values or emotions: they are the natural spirits of the land. They are the spirits of the forests, the valleys, and the moorlands. They can infuse a human with madness, or simply harass one who stumbles upon their land.

When this card appears in a reading, it can either warn of such faerie interference in human life, or it can, for a magician, indicate a faerie being who is willing to work with the human. If this is the case, then tread very carefully: these beings can be very difficult if not worked with properly.

It can also represent the forces of nature and the land around you, when those forces are having some influence on you. If this card appears in a magical reading, ensure that you are working magically in a way that is conducive to the land, plants, trees, and creatures around you, and that you are not inadvertently causing conflict through your work.

Mundane Divination: Someone who is unreliable, who can cause trouble, or who suffers from mental instability. It can also indicate a period of unease or unbalance in the mental or physical health of the subject.

BLOOD ANCESTOR

Blood Ancestor

Blood Ancestor is the primal ancestor and the shoulders upon which we stand as human beings. This card connects us to the root of all we have come from, a root with which we can still connect.

The card can also indicate a Sleeper, an ancient human who chose at their death—usually a ritual slaying—to refrain from going back into the cycle of life and death, and to stay in the land and sleep. By staying in the land they dream the future, and they commune with the land, the creatures, and the humans. Cultures all around the world have ancient ritual sleepers. They are part and parcel of the living world, the tap-root of all that is human. Be aware, however, that some later sleepers in some cultures were forced into the role against their will, as sacrificial sleepers, and that is a different dynamic altogether.

When this card appears in a reading, whatever its topic, it shows the magician that an ancient ancestor is still sleeping in the land and active, or a distant blood ancestor is working in the orbit of the magician, usually to protect and guide them, though sometimes to interfere. They will speak through the land, and through the magician's dreams and visions.

Do not assume that such an appearance is always for the magician's benefit: sometimes these awakenings happen when the land is in extreme danger, or a massive change is coming, or the line of skills or bloodline that the ancestors are the roots of is at risk. The magician could simply be a pawn in a much bigger game: remember, it's not always about you! But whenever this card appears, pay close attention to its position in the reading, and be very aware that something important is happening.

It can also indicate, depending on its position and the question, that some inherited dynamic or physical feature of the magician has its roots deep in their ancestral or magical lineage. The Blood Ancestor is also connected to the 'Developing Ones' who sleep in the caverns of the Duat in Egyptian funeral texts. The card represents a being who keeps a spiritual and/or energetic presence in the land of the living while they rest in the Underworld. This card is about deep roots, inherited patterns, and those ancients who went before you.

Mundane Divination: Inherited dynamics, skills, or genetics.

GHOST

Ghost

The Ghost tells us about people who have died but whose spirits continue to wander in and out of our world. They are not lying asleep in the earth as an ancestor, and nor have they walked through death and towards rebirth. These are the people who get stuck or wait around for a variety of reasons, and who continuously try to connect with the living.

This card depicts a woman veiled and bathed in moonlight. Unable to see clearly, the shade operates more and more in the realm of the imagination and emotions. This is a card of illusions, ghosts, and fractured sight.

When someone dies, it is expected for them to try and connect with the living for a short while, but in normal circumstances their spirit moves on within a few weeks. However, when someone is trapped or has refused to move for some reason, they continue to cling to the world of the living. The longer they cling, the more they begin to lose the sense of who they were: they slowly become shells of themselves. These shells make great vessels for parasitic beings who step in and operate through the ghost, evoking emotive reactions in humans and feeding off the energy of that emotive reaction.

This card can also appear in readings when someone who is now dead is trying to join in the work of the magician, or to bask in the energy and path ahead of the work. Such situations should always be attended to, but approached with care and balance: hostile magic has no place here, and the magician should gently but firmly insist that they move along.

The card can also appear when a dead magician or priest has come into your life pattern at a critical point to guard and guide you. It is important to walk your own path, but sometimes help is needed. Just do not become dependent on them or acknowledge them: do your job and let them do theirs. Interacting with them opens a pathway for energy to go back and forth, which attracts parasites.

This card can literally mean a ghost, but more often it tells of illusions, beings, or spirits masquerading as something they are not, or of not seeing someone as they truly are. Whereas the Luna card tells of our own illusions, the Ghost card tells us of beings that are not as they seem. Take this card as a warning to step back and reassess: you are missing something and are not seeing someone or some being for what they are.

Mundane Divination: Someone is not as they seem, or some hidden person in your life is affecting you from the shadows. It can also literally mean a haunting.

PARASITE

Parasite

A parasite is a being that feeds off the energy and emotions of others. This order of beings is often problematic for magicians, as parasites can dress up and pretend to be something they are not to get a human to connect with them.

Parasites will often encourage a person to behave in out-of-character ways. The parasite may cause an exaggeration of some disturbing emotion or generate physical, sexual, or violent impulses. This card can also appear where there is some potential for illness that is essentially parasitical: a worm infection, a virus (they live within the host for the lifespan of the host), or indeed any number of parasitical insects and vermin that can infest the body.

The card can also represent a person who is parasitical by nature, an energy vampire. Often these people are not aware that they drain energy from others. They will leave a social gathering feeling wonderful, while everyone else is drained and exhausted. The card has to be read in relation to the question and its position in the layout for its meaning to be understood.

When this card appears, it is either a warning that something or someone is feeding off or affecting your energies, or a warning that a being is encouraging you to do something or behave in a way that keeps a food source going. By identifying the food source (hate, anger, fear, sexual arousal, illusions), the magician can work with their own emotional discipline to starve the parasite out. When the reading is about a building or place, it can indicate that the place itself is parasited and needs cleaning up.

Mundane Divination: This card can be a health warning: something may be draining you. Or someone may be using you to get something they want. It can indicate 'hangers on,' people who profess to be your friend but only wish to take from you; or it can indicate people or places that drain you. Such parasitical situations are not dangerous, but they can be exhausting and time consuming to deal with.

Chapter VI

The Physical Realm: Powers and Dynamics That Flow Through Humanity

We are not separated from spirit, we are in it.

— Plotinus

The cards in this chapter represent human personalities, human powers such as premonitions and abilities, and human patterns of behaviour. While these may express through us, they can at times have their sources in the inner worlds and in fate dynamics. The cards in this section can directly indicate a person or a type of person, but they can also indicate a quality or dynamic of an individual or group. They can represent things that affect our minds and bodies, as well as certain magical dynamics used to affect or manipulate a person or group.

PREMONITION

Premonition

This card depicts an old Celtic magical figure called the Bean-sídhe (faerie woman), also known as the Washer By The Ford. In Irish mythology, the Bean-sídhe appears the morning of a battle and washes the clothes of men who are about to die. She gives to whomever she appears a warning about impending doom.

Magicians train in a variety of skills. One is divination, and another is the use of magic to elicit change. When this card appears in a reading, it warns of some potential disaster that can be averted. The card's position in the layout can indicate the source of the potential disaster, and this information can help the magician head off the oncoming problem and sidestep the impact.

First, note this card's position in the reading. Then begin reading to identify the potential problem's cause, the area of life where it will strike, and your options for avoiding it.

Sometimes these warnings are about the literal death of someone. There are two reasons why a magician would be shown the death of someone. The first is as a warning when the death can be avoided and it is up to the magician to work out how to sidestep it. The second is when the death is unavoidable and the magician needs to work actively with the person fated to die either before, at, or immediately after their death.

It can also appear when a magical working is unbalanced and could lead to disaster or illness, or when a destructive situation looms on the horizon that you need to spot and avoid. If this card turns up in a health reading, then it is telling you that if you do not take action, sickness or weakness is likely to manifest. It can also appear in health readings and magical readings when the person is depressed and has feelings of impending doom. If the rest of the reading (and subsequent twelve month readings) look fine, then it points to a purely emotional situation that may need medical or psychological help. The card can also appear when a person is overworked and overstretched and needs to cut back, rest, and regenerate.

Mundane Divination: Something potentially unpleasant, some life situation, event, or illness is on the horizon, and needs to be identified and dealt with to avoid it. The card can also indicate a person who has the 'second sight,' who can see future events in flashes—usually disastrous events. In general, this is a warning card representing a threat that can be avoided if you use your instincts and common sense.

GLAMOUR

Glamour

Being sucked in by Glamour is a major issue for magicians. This can take many forms; the common denominator is being seduced by something that is not real, that has no power content. The basic meaning of this card is "not all is as it seems." For magicians, this trap can manifest in various ways: the quest for grades, the wish for fashionable magical toys, the lure of self-importance, or the feeling that ritual costumes, status, and an altar cluttered with purchased magical objects is what makes a magician.

All these things are hurdles that the magician must overcome to access real power. There is nothing wrong with any of these things, so long as you understand that none of them are actually magic. (And if you enjoy them only for their own sake, then they will not affect your magic.) Often, though, this card appears when someone still caught in their first flush of excitement at magic's strange symbols, obscure language, and secret signs, has developed a feeling of self-importance.

When this card appears in a reading, it warns that you are fooling yourself and being seduced by some glamour that will ultimately destroy you if you do not recognize it for what it is.

A major part of the development of a magician is to *know thyself*, which includes not being glamoured and knowing your weaknesses rather than indulging in them with a head full of excuses. Attend to this card's position in a reading: it will give you a clue about the type of glamour misleading or seducing you. This card can also point to lies—either telling lies or being told lies. It is a card of illusions, of distractions, and of not paying attention to something that could be critically important.

Mundane Divination: When this card appears, you are being fooled by something or someone, or you are fooling yourself. By being taken in by a glamour, you are being distracted from seeing the reality of some situation, or your focus is being diverted away from where it needs to be.

TEMPTATION

Temptation

Magic holds a mirror up to our true selves, making us aware of our weaknesses so that we can address them. We all have weaknesses, and part of the process in magic is to become aware of them, analyse why they have such a hold on us, then act on that information to strengthen ourselves. Temptation has as many faces as humanity itself.

Part of the process of magical development is to address our issues, not through therapy but by being truthful with ourselves. This in turn enables us to create our own boundaries, ones we know we need, and to live by them. As with all magic, this is not about morality or social acceptance, but about knowing our weak spots. When you are up to your eyebrows in deep inner magic, any weakness has the potential to be manipulated and used by inner beings in order to destroy us.

When this card appears in a reading, its position will indicate the type of temptation to which you are being subjected, and the cards around it, or at the reading's conclusion, will show the outcome of not tackling it. This card warns you about some weakness of yours that needs working on. Identify it, understand why it is there and how it came about, and be truthful with yourself about the best way to tackle it.

It can also represent a weakness in health that puts the magician at risk if they are doing heavy work. If you are clear that you know your own inherent weaknesses and are properly prepared for powerful magic, and this card still turns up in your reading, then check through divination whether it represents some physical weakness, or even a weakness in the magical patterns or structure with which you are working. Forewarned is forearmed, and if you know that there is a weakness somewhere and have identified it, then you are better placed to take it into account when doing magical work.

Mundane Divination: Similar to the magical meanings of this card, the mundane meaning highlights a weakness in the person or situation being read about. This could be an emotional, physical, or energetic weakness, or even simply making a bad decision.

SCAPEGOAT

Scapegoat

The Scapegoat appears when someone or something is trying to shift the consequences of an action onto another person. Magically this can be used in a very nasty and powerful way, and should this card turn up in a reading it would indicate the dodging of consequences, or the transplanting of a destructive fate onto another person. The Scapegoat also appears when a person has not learned their lesson and has tried to shift the consequences or blame for an unbalanced act onto someone else. On a mundane level this may seem a minor thing, but for a magician scapegoating can have an extremely powerful impact.

Magic works through balance and the harmonic flow of power. When the magician inadvertently disrupts this flow, the consequences—whether major or minor—serve to teach the magician. This is not about learning any moral lessons, but about learning the simple dynamic of cause and effect.

This card can appear in readings when the magician is either consciously dodging the results of their actions, or is unconsciously trying to shift a consequence onto someone else. It can also indicate magical scapegoating, and warns that a person is carrying a burden that is not theirs.

This card can also represent load-sharing, your energy being taken up by another person, place, or event. Perhaps the magician is a natural empath and their energies are supporting a child, partner, sibling, etc. This sort of natural load-sharing will subside once there is no longer a need for it. When a magician is involved in long-term magical projects or ones with far-reaching consequences, their energy can also be taken up and used by the magical pattern. (In fact your magical work always flows through you, and this can affect you every time it triggers.) This manifests as a temporary loss of energy while the pattern is active.

If you experience such a loss of energy and this card shows up, then it would be wise to check through divination to see whether your energy is supporting your work or your loved ones, or supporting some world event. In these cases, the temporary energy loss will resolve in its own time.

Mundane Divination: Being scapegoated in a situation, or carrying burden or blame. It can also show the positive carrying of burdens to relieve the sufferings of others. The context will indicate whether this card should be interpreted positively or negatively.

DISEASE

Disease

This is a natural, conscious, destructive power that flows through the physical realm and literally brings disease. Disease appears when there is some imbalance that can trigger degeneration and destruction. We all get sick, and usually we get better with time and help. But the Disease card can also warn of deeper imbalances, say in a genetic line, a person, or a lifestyle.

When this card appears in a reading, it may simply mean that the magician will get sick. If the rest of the reading progresses well, then any such illness will be overcome in its own time, and may be of little long-term consequence. However, if this card appears in a powerful position and is followed by problematic or destructive cards, then it can indicate that the magician needs to reassess how they work or live their life, and also ensure they get proper medical care.

It tells us that something, somewhere, is out of balance for the individual, which puts them at risk of disease. The imbalance could be anywhere: too much intense magical work, living in an unbalanced place, or eating the wrong foods. If this card appears, then think carefully about the various aspects of your life and see if anything can be adjusted to support your health rather than threaten it.

This card can also indicate the *magical disease*. This is often a difficult illness that is not fatal, but which can be problematic and requires careful long-term strategies for maintaining the body and energy. The 'magical disease' has been known about for thousands of years. It is often a long trial period in a magician's life that pushes them and yet limits them to polish them into something very special: their health energy is diminished to release it as a resource for extreme magical development. Magicians who suffer from the magical disease must learn to self-limit, to care for their body and inner energy, and to withdraw into seclusion as much as possible. Through such self-limitation, they will learn to cope with the deficit in their health energy and properly manage their more abundant magical energy. It is all about learning to keep a good balance.

Mundane Divination: When this card appears, it can indicate a period of sickness, or warn that a sickness is coming. Most often it indicates minor illnesses of short duration, and warns you to look after yourself and let your body heal.

MAGICAL ATTACK

Magical Attack

This card can indicate a magical attack aimed at a person, place, thing, or group. It can also indicate hostility from nature spirits, deities, or hostile energies.

When this card appears with regard to an actual magical attack, the magician is either somehow involved in it, or is on its receiving end. This card warns particularly of the folly of falling into the trap of mounting any sort of counterattack the original assailant: this would open—and keep open—a line of energy that can then flow back and forth. Such a connection will keep the hostilities going energetically, and will attract parasites with a vested interest in keeping the 'war' going. This card often appears in a reading along with the Parasite card, as the two are close bedfellows.

If this card appears, then it is either a warning for the magician to cease some hostile action, as they are getting themselves in an energetic tangle, or an indication that they or the reading's subject are under attack.

The best action a magician can take when under attack is to detach emotionally from the situation, scrape the magic off and dump it, and ignore where the magic came from. This will trigger a deeper magical dynamic of the Grindstone and the Unraveller: the magician grows strong and learns a great deal from constantly removing what has been thrown at them, and the attacker slowly unravels as their pour all their energy into unsuccessful attacks.

When this card appears in a reading, look closely at its position (where the attack is coming from), what cards are around it, and what the future holds. Look at the outcome in a second reading to see what would happen if you employ the simple, drawn-out, but effective strategy of just removing the magic each time it is thrown at you.

We all want justice, but by seeking human justice we can upset certain deeper balances that we are unaware of. By simply taking the magic off each time, the attacked magician stays fine and dandy; and there can be no greater punishment for an arrogant, attacking magician than for them to realize that they are ineffectual and essentially without real power.

If this card instead represents hostile violence from nature spirits, ancestors, deities, and so forth, then it would be wise to use divination to find out what, if anything, you have done to trigger such a response, and take action to remedy it or avoid it. In such circumstances, there is no protection in magic that would work strongly enough to override such hostility directly: it would be wiser and better to find out what is causing the problem, and attend to the problem itself. The card can appear when you are at 'odds' with your surroundings, or simply that there is a hostile energy that it working itself out from the land.

If the card appears in a health reading, then it can indicate a 'fight' going on in your body between your immune system and an invader, or your immune system and your own body. It indicates inflammation, an immune response that brings pain and suffering, or your body/energy/spirit trying to fight something. Use divination to further pinpoint the cause and take the appropriate action: medicines, etc.

Mundane Divination: Hostilities, heated arguments, and attacks that could be physical emotional or energetic. Use yes/no layouts (Tree of Life is a good one, featured in the layouts chapter) to pinpoint the details of how the attack will affect you and what is the best course of action to take.

On Good Friday that event happened in Caithness that a man whose name was Daurrud went out.

He saw folk riding twelve together to a bower, and there they were all lost to his sight.

He went to that bower and looked in through a window slit that was in it, and saw that there were women inside, and they had set up a loom.

Men's heads were the weights, but men's entrails were the warp and weft, a sword was the shuttle, and the reels were arrows. They sang these songs, and he learnt them by heart:

"See! warp is stretched
For warriors' fall,
Lo! weft in loom Tis wet with blood;
Now fight foreboding,
'Neath friends' swift fingers,
Our grey woof waxeth
With war's alarms,
Our warp bloodred,
Our weft corseblue. This woof is y-woven
With entrails of men,
This warp is hardweighted
With heads of the slain,
Spears blood-besprinkled
For spindles we use,
Our loom ironbound,
And arrows our reels;
With swords for our shuttles
This war-woof we work;
So weave we, weird sisters,
Our warwinning woof."

— *Darraðarljoð* (*The Battle Song of the Valkyries*)
(Extract from the Icelandic *Njal's Saga*)

GIVER OF GIFTS

Giver of Gifts

This is a minor card that indicates giving and receiving gifts. The gifts can come from fellow humans, beings, or deities around the magician. The card may indicate that the best course of action would be to give a gift, or that the magician should tend to a being, deity, or person by ensuring that they have what they need.

The deeper aspect of this card is ensuring that *needs*, not wants, are met so that everyone can move forward. As a minor card, it is often read in relation to the question and the other cards that fall around it. It is a card of checks and balances, of ensuring that the scales of energy and substance are balanced. The appearance of this card tells you that you will receive what you need. If you are not in need, then it could be telling you to help someone.

Mundane Divination: The giving or receiving of what is needed. This can be resources like food or money, or property, or a gift that makes a difference to your life. In a health reading it can also represent necessary medicine: being given what you need in order to get better.

BAILIFF

Bailiff

This card is the polar opposite of the Giver of Gifts: the Bailiff takes what is due, what needs taking. When this card appears in a reading it can signify loss, having to pay dues, or having something stolen. Usually it indicates some loss that restores balance, however expensive or painful this loss may be.

It can also indicate a fate pattern that has been taken from you as it no longer serves a purpose. In some magical readings, it can indicate the angel of death—one who gets involved when the fate span of a person, place, or event is finished. It can also appear in health readings when someone is ill and is not getting the proper treatment, or the illness is threatening to go down a bad road: the angel of death starts circling the fate of the person.

If this card shows up in a health or life reading and the person is ill, and the card is placed with the Death card or Bridge of Death, then it is a warning to reassess treatment. If the change of direction of treatment is right, then this card should either vanish entirely from the readings or move to a healthier position where the Bailiff takes away the illness, not the person.

Mundane Divination: Paying dues, paying fines, necessary or unavoidable loss.

WISE TEACHER

Wise Teacher

This card indicates that someone is coming into the magician's life who will be a wise and honourable teacher, helper, and friend. Often wise teachers appear in our lives in unusual forms and when we least expect them. They are not obvious teachers; most often they appear as a nice person willing to help you. But through their help they teach you a great deal about yourself.

Wise teachers often pass through a magician's life unnoticed, bringing subtle but important changes. The voices of the gods sometimes speak through them, and if we pay attention to them then we can learn a great deal about ourselves and the deeper aspects of magic.

When this card appears in a reading, it indicates that someone close to the reading's subject matter is a potential guide or teacher and is working in the magician's interests. It can also indicate a teacher in general. There are occasions, depending on the question of the reading, where this card can indicate old age or maturing into older age, particularly if you are looking at a lifespan.

It can also represent your own wisdom that is gained from experience. True wisdom comes from the hardships of learning, and through that learning, you gain experience and therefore wisdom.

Mundane Divination: An older teacher, or wisdom that comes with age. It can also indicate an elder in a family or group.

FELLOWSHIP

Fellowship

This card indicates fellowship, and can relate to some group the magician is involved with. It represents a collaborative group of like-minded people. Sometimes we are not aware of the fellowship around us; sometimes it is a group scattered across the globe but kept connected through the stream of magic.

When this card appears, it can indicate that the magician is either working with, or will soon connect with, a fellowship of magicians or like-minded people.

Its deeper meaning in a magical reading is that though the reader may feel alone, they are not: they are becoming part of a wider fellowship of magicians or magical people. As time passes, the distance narrows between the fellows, and the bonds between them tighten. This card signals the birth of a magical family, the bonds of friendship, and the powers of fellowship.

It can also indicate an inner fellowship, a group of inner contacts or spirits who are guiding you, protecting you, and working with you. When this card appears in a magical reading, pay special attention to it, and be aware of the ways that the inner contacts are trying to communicate with you. Be aware of them around you, and respect their willingness to protect and guide you.

This card can also represent a group of people working collectively *against* your best interests, and at worst, mounting an attack against you. This can be indicated when this card appears, badly placed, in a reading that warns that you may be in danger or involved in some sort of conflict.

Mundane Divination: When this card appears in a mundane reading, it can indicate friends and family who are quietly supporting you or watching over you. It shows friendships, companions, family, and a group of like-minded people with your best interests at heart. If this card is badly placed, then it could indicate a group of people coming together to harm or interfere with you in some way. Read this card in context.

COMMUNICATION

Communication

This card indicates writing, the transcription of knowledge, and the keeping of records. When this card appears in a reading it indicates the need to write, to study, and to work with written communication. This could be magical writing, or it could indicate the importance of writing down one's knowledge and experience to ensure its future survival.

It can also represent someone who works as a 'scribe.' In general, however, it indicates the written word and its importance in magic.

Occasionally it represents communication from inner contacts. It can appear with the Oracle card when there is a strong need for you to be aware of such attempted communication, and to act accordingly.

Mundane Divination: Letters, telephone calls, communication of importance, learning, writing, study. If this card appears in a mundane reading, then it can herald an important communication that needs your full attention—often one that is subtle and easily missed. The card's appearance tells you to pay attention to communications around you, or that some form of communication around you is of greater importance than it first appears to be.

SECLUSION

Seclusion

Seclusion is a straightforward card with a simple but important message: *you need to withdraw.* Whatever the reading's subject, this card tells us that someone or something needs to withdraw, wait, take time out, and rest. It shows the need to wait and be still. It can indicate a period of withdrawal needed to heal and recover from something, or a need to stay away from the bustle of everyday life.

Sometimes a magician must take themselves out of the daily connections of everyday life, such as social gatherings, going into busy cities, and so forth. At times, certain energies damaging to a magician can collect or sweep through an area: the magician must stay home, away from everyone, and keep a low profile until the disruptive energy recedes.

Mundane Divination: A need for seclusion, healing, withdrawal, and introspection.

Chapter VII

The Physical Realm:
The Elemental Magical Tools

Men who are devoid of the power of spiritual perception are unable to recognize anything that cannot be seen externally.

— Paracelsus

This short chapter introduces the four magical tools and their elements, and demonstrates how these tools can speak to us through divination. The cards teach us about the powers and dynamics of the tools and their respective elements. When they appear in readings, they can either literally indicate the tool's use or action, or they can represent its associated power flowing into the magician's life. Sometimes the power of the tools flows naturally around us, and sometimes their associated elements and contacts can become major players in our life and fate.

LIMITER

Limiter: Air, East

The appearance of the sword, the Limiter, in a magical reading can be good or bad. It has no inherent moral or emotive quality: it is simply an expression of a pure magical element. It is a blade; it is also a breath and an utterance. It is the magical power of air.

The Limiter is the magical sword that limits power, slowing it so that the power can be worked with by a human. The Limiter is a lower octave of the Grindstone, one of the angels of creative manifestation. It is connected with the magical direction of east, the power of magical utterance, and the element of air.

When this card appears in a magical reading, it is about guarding, limiting, or boundaries. It can indicate the need to work with the magical sword to contain some power, to hold something back, or to limit something.

If the magical question is about directions and elements, then this card would represent the powers of the east, air, and utterance. If the reading is about a magical attack, then it could indicate that someone is using hostile limiting powers or utterances against the magician to limit them.

It can also represent some active limiting dynamic in the situation, something being limited out of necessity or through actions. In a health reading, too, it shows something being limited: here it may represent something as simple as the person not getting enough sleep or food. But wherever the card falls, it brings the power of limitation with it, and can be a clear indicator of something not flowing.

Mundane Divination: Limitation, suppression, withholding, slowing something down. Perhaps natural limitation in reaction to something, such as a limb being limited because of injury or illness, or a life path being limited. This may be happening for the person's own good, or it may be holding them back unnecessarily: the card has to be read in context of the question and layout.

STAFF OF THE GODS

Staff of the Gods: Fire, South

The magical staff or wand is a passive tool that is upheld by the magician to connect with the power of fire, potential, the south, and the future. It is called the Staff of the Gods because its power should never be wielded actively by the magician: its power is for the gods alone.

We humans have a very limited understanding of what lies ahead of us in the future. Even with the power of prophecy, there is much we can misunderstand. We often do not get the bigger picture. For an inexperienced magician, wielding the Staff of the Gods actively can be more trouble that it is worth. Later, as an adept, the magician learns to work with the staff. Even then it is not used as a tool; rather the magician develops a relationship with the companion spirit who works through the staff or wand. Together they work as a team, and the adept learns about the serpent power that flows through the staff, which operates as a guardian and an *Opener of the Ways.*

The appearance of this card in a magical reading tells of the creative fire of the potential future, and that the gods are actively working with the magician to open the way forward for some potential future. This card asks you to trust the gods. It says, "the future is being formed: you do your bit, and we will do ours."

It can also represent the pure element of fire, and so can warn about fire magic being used that may harm the magician or the subject of the reading. The power represented by this card is volatile. It must be respected, and it can work for or against the magician. If this card is badly placed in a reading, then it may be warning you that too much fire power is flowing into a situation, and you should rebalance your work or take action to rebalance the 'fire' in the situation.

Where it appears in the reading will tell you where the power it represents is most active, or how far into the future it is working. If it falls in an Underworld position, then it shows that power being taken away from the life or situation being read about.

Mundane Divination: A lot of fire power flowing into a situation. Fate has been triggered strongly. There is need to take a firm but calm stance. Power, action, an opening of the future path ahead.

REGENERATOR

Regenerator: Water, West

The Regenerator is the magical vessel that carries regeneration—its natural power—and dispenses it where it is needed. The appearance of this card indicates renewal, growth, regeneration, and rebirth. It can also indicate the element of water and the magical act of dispensing; or it can indicate the need to work magically with water or with the magical vessel, either for the body or for the land. Its magical direction is west, and its power is ultimately one of completion.

The appearance of this card can herald the end of a long period of illness, weakness, undue stress, or burden. It promises a change in such a cycle, and a time to come that will bring energy, vitality, and regeneration to a situation or person.

Mundane Divination: Health, energy, renewal, and regeneration are the key words to be applied to a person, place, or situation. It marks the end of struggle and the beginning of growth, the spring at the end of a long winter. It is the magical cauldron of regeneration that gifts life, health, and happiness.

FOUNDATION

Foundation: Earth, North

Foundation is the earth power that we stand upon, the power that roots us to life and the land. As a foundation it upholds us, gives us strength, and allows us to draw on ancient knowledge and wisdom. The roots of Foundation are deep within the Underworld and the past. It is that foundation that propels us forward into the future.

The appearance of Foundation in a magical reading signifies earth magic, land spirits, or working magically with rock/stone. It can act as a shield, as a container (rocks, particularly large ones, are good for putting beings in when you run out of other places to put them), or as a guardian.

Depending on where this card falls and what the question is, this card can indicate the need to be aware of earth magic or land spirits, or the need to use rock/stone as a magical tool, container, anchor, or guardian. It can also indicate that the magic in question must be rooted and anchored in a foundation if it is to be stable.

It can also indicate that something has deep roots in the past which enable it to survive into the future. It can show the foundation of a new system, a new culture, a new life path, all of which have emerged from the past. It can be the root of something, the anchor, the parent, and even a literal foundation stone placed for some magical or physical construction: the rock upon which the temple is built.

Mundane Divination: The beginning of a long term project, literally the 'founding' of something. The foundations of a building, the source of a tribe, the root of a mountain, a patch of land that is a focal point for something. In a personal or health reading, it can show where the strength of a person or situation comes from, or that someone is moving to a more stable phase in their lives. Its key words are: anchor, stability, source, roots, and settlement.

Chapter VIII

The Physical Realm:
The Cards of Humanity

I understand that the word 'occult' means hidden, but surely that is not meant to be the final state of all this information, hidden forever. I don't see why there is any need to further obscure things that are actually lucid and bright.

— Alan Moore

The Cards of Humanity look widely and deeply at various archetypal characters who may cross paths with a magician. The gender of a card in this group reflects the biological sex from which its personality or quality generally—but not exclusively—emerges: there is fluidity here.

These cards can also indicate types of magicians, as well as reflect where you are on your own magical and mystical path. All these archetypes are inherent within all of us: discovering how and when they emerge can prompt one's self-development, self-reflection, and personal evolution.

HIEROPHANT

Hierophant

The Hierophant is the bridge in humanity between the outer and inner worlds. Hierophants can be male or female and are not necessarily religious, but they are always mystical and magical.

We often think of a Hierophant as a head of a magical order. This is an incorrect assumption. The role of a Hierophant is to bridge the Inner Mysteries and guide others as they seek a deeper understanding of the powers of Divinity and the inner worlds. Such an act cannot be defined by a religion, a magical path, or a culture: a Hierophant's work transcends all boundaries and structures erected by humanity.

The Hierophant card indicates that such a person or power dynamic is drawing near the individual or situation being read about. It can also indicate that a human inner contact of considerable power and learning is about to instigate a period of teaching in the life and magical work of the subject.

This card may also indicate that the magician will shortly undergo a period of major development in their magical and spiritual understanding.

A magician who walks the path towards the power of the Hierophant leaves behind all comfortable, safe, and dependable structures. Such a magician can no longer depend on the stability of a magical lodge or group, or the safety of a religion: all these structures are limited in their understanding of the Inner Mysteries, and the Hierophant must step away from such comforts.

So the appearance of this card could indicate moving away from comfortable, known expressions of spirituality. The life of a Hierophant ceases to be the life of an individual and instead becomes a beacon of the Mysteries, a life of service and hard work in the constant magical and spiritual evolution of the people. It is a card of responsibility, service, teaching, and upholding the Mysteries.

Mundane Divination: A religious leader, senior teacher, or professor.

UNION

Union

This archetypal tarot card shows the union between two people. This can be a union of bodies, minds, souls, or all the above. This card tells us of relationships and how we relate to those around us. It can indicate a relationship or a magical partnership. Where this card falls tells us how this union will affect the life or situation of the subject.

It can also indicate an agreement between two people to work towards a mutual goal, or a period of magical cooperation between two people who work as a unit. It can also indicate where two powers are working together in union to bring something to fruition.

Mundane Divination: Partnership, union, marriage, contracts, agreements.

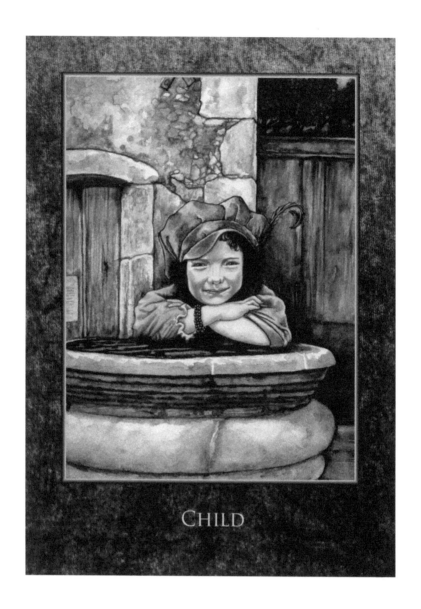

CHILD

Child

The Child is a simple card that often indicates a literal child. Like all children, it is full of potential but has not yet formed a full personality. When this card appears in a magical reading, it shows a child coming into the magician's orbit. Where the card falls tells us the role the child will play in the context of the reading. It can also indicate an adult who is as yet lacking in life or magical experience: someone who is *as* a child.

The child can also be read as feeling young, having a new lease of life, having youthful energy, or starting something new that will grow and mature if nurtured properly.

Mundane Divination: A child, youthful energy, a new project.

ELDER

Elder

This card indicates that an old person, or someone with the wisdom and understanding of an older person—some souls are old souls—is influencing the situation. As with all the people cards, it must be read in relation to where it falls in the layout and the cards that surround it.

We often think we know better than our elders—and that may be true in many respects. But there is no substitute for experience, and wisdom wears many faces. This card can appear when you are engaging with your own deep wisdom and knowledge, or when there is someone nearby with those qualities.

In health readings it can indicate the ageing process, ageing-like or age-related symptoms of an illness, or someone feeling old and tired. The card has to do with wisdom gained from long experience, and the burdens of age. Just when your mind starts to mature deeply, your body starts to weaken and wear out. In fate readings this card can indicate a long life ahead into old age, as well as those responsibilities that can come with age.

Mundane Divination: An elder or elderly person; the wear and tear of age.

IDIOT

Idiot

This card represents total stupidity and emptiness.

The moon shines down on an apprentice magician who is supported only by their books, and who is ignoring the warning of the cat that is desperately trying to save them. A fire burns around them, unnoticed and ignored.

When this card appears in a reading, it warns of some stupidity that can lead to disaster. It can indicate that you are doing something stupid or planning to do so, or that some action will have a stupid outcome. It is telling you not to be an idiot! It can also stand for the answer 'no,' as well as 'zero,' 'nothing,' and 'empty.'

Mundane Divination: The Fool, foolishness, emptiness, nothing. Something is no longer necessary or of any consequence. Your reading is unnecessary, or the question itself is foolish. This is not a frivolous card: the Idiot warns that you are walking down a path of foolishness that can lead to destructive or difficult outcomes.

Male Powers and Qualities

Note: The following five cards refer to generally male magical powers and qualities. But gender is never quite as straightforward as we think, and we all have male and female powers within us, so allow some fluidity in your divination.

OCCULTIST

Occultist

The Occultist indicates a male or female magician whose work has to do with control and manipulation, and who is often lacking in ethics and mature reasoning. This card may be good or bad in a reading, depending on how this person is applying this dynamic. This stage of a magician's life tells us of the giddy sense of power that working with a controlling dynamic can give a magician. But it can be a false power if not approached properly, and it can severely limit the magical horizon of anyone walking such a path.

When this card appears, it can indicate that the magician in question is currently at this early stage of their development. How things will unfold can be seen in the layout positions that tell of the future. It can also indicate, depending on the layout, a struggle with a magician of this level.

The Occultist often represents younger or immature magicians, ones who have not yet been put through the grinder of deeper magic. They tend to be more theory than practice, and wield their magic to manipulate.

Mundane Divination: This card can represent someone who is manipulative, who holds some authority but is not particularly wise or mature. It can also represent manipulation, power games, passive-aggressive behaviour, or simply a wish to try and control a situation. It can be a warning to watch your behaviour carefully, or to watch carefully someone in your life who could be manipulating situations behind the scenes. It is not always a 'bad' card; it may simply represent someone trying to find their feet in the world who has not yet learned maturity. It can also represent bureaucratic, senseless red tape that needs to be dealt with, or people trying to play power games with you. Do not be taken in by such people: be firm, honest, and allow them a chance to show the better side of their personality.

LEADER

The Leader

As the magician learns to move forward and surrender their need for control, a different, more mature power comes to them. The Leader is a man with a solid grounding in magic who has learned to wield that magic for the benefit of the land and the people. The Leader rides the White Horse, the spirit that carries humans between the worlds, and he has the Limiter strapped to his hip.

Before him is the Mountain: the challenges of overcoming dogma, fixed thinking, and overly structured religion and magic. All these barriers to Divinity create what we perceive in inner vision as a mountain.

Though the Leader is a highly skilled magical adept, he still rides the White Horse instead of walking through the Inner Realms alone. The Leader understands that if he is to serve in both the outer and inner worlds, he must be firmly rooted in both. This means voluntarily limiting his own energetic magical resources (Pots of Resources) so that the more practical resources of energy are still available to him.

Though he appears richly dressed, this does not indicate great wealth or lavish tastes; it tells us about his careful balancing of his energetic pots. Self-limiting his magical power lets him also wield material power: both are kept in balance and check by the Limiter.

When this card appears in a magical reading it tells us of an adept, male or female, working with this balance of power and service, who operates in all worlds equally. With such status comes great burdens and responsibility: it is the Leader who carries the greatest burden, and the Limiter is constantly ready to strike him down should he abuse his gifts, his power, or his people. This card indicates a leader or someone, male or female, who carries this sort of responsibility.

Mundane Divination: This card can represent an authority figure in the reader's life, one with some power over the reader, or one who can offer true guidance, help, and resources if necessary. The person could be male or female, and it can also represent a quality within the reader that they need to express wisely.

MAN OF NATURE

The Man of Nature

The Man of Nature is a magical stage, a bit like the Occultist, that many magicians pass through and learn from. The Man of Nature is close to all that is wild and rejects the structures of civilization, instead focusing their magic on the upkeep of the land, the animals, and the land spirits.

During this phase, the magician learns about the intricate balance of nature in real terms. Nature is not cute, whimsical, or romantic: it is a harsh balancing act that does not care what is in your heart. It is about predator and prey, and the creative and destructive forces of the elements. And it has no time for wishful thinking: nature demands understanding and respect.

It is very important for a magician to connect fully with and understand the natural world around them, as one of the roles of Adept is to oversee 'the Garden' and learn how to operate in conjunction with nature rather than in conflict with it. This will also give the magician a deeper understanding of inner world dynamics, and of how we humans operate on the planet.

The stage of connecting with nature is vital in magical training, and it is a major part of understanding power dynamics. But it can also become a romantic trap. The media has fed us many stories of 'Merlin' and shamans who live in harmony with the animals: these are skewed fantasies to which city-dwellers are often drawn in an effort to reconnect with a major part of their selves. Like all good stories, these have elements of the truth, but that truth is drowned in sentiment and ignorance.

The degenerate side of the Man of Nature is this failure to face up to the stark reality of nature. Instead, the magician loses themselves in a fantasy world created from fragments of truths dressed in a hide of wishful thinking. Just as the Occultist operates from a place of control, so the Man of Nature functions from a place of no control and no focus, and instead indulges in wild, impulsive behaviour which can quickly descend into madness.

This card must be read in the context of its position in the layout and the question at hand. It can indicate a healthy period of learning from nature and a magical connection to the land, or it can indicate a foolish adherence to a 'wild path' that holds delusion.

This card can also appear in readings when natural land and animal spirits are trying to connection with the magician, or are surrounding them. It can herald a time of deep inner connection with the spirits of the land, but it is also a warning to not get lost in that connection.

Mundane Divination: This card can represent a man close to nature or working on the land or with animals. It can also appear when the reader needs to connect better with nature and understand it better. It is the card that represents our deep connection to the land an animals around us, and reminds us that we are a part of all that, and should not forget it.

Merlin called his companions out from the battle and bade them bury the brothers in a richly coloured chapel; and he bewailed the men and did not cease to pour out laments, and he strewed dust on his hair and rent his garments, and prostrate on the ground rolled now hither and now thither. Peredur strove to console him and so did the nobles and princes, but he would not be comforted nor put up with their beseeching words. He had now lamented for three whole days and had refused food, so great was the grief that consumed him.

Then when he had filled the air with so many and so great complaints, new fury seized himand he departed secretly, and fled to the woods not wishing to be seen as he fled. He entered the wood and rejoiced to lie hidden under the ash trees; he marvelled at the wild beasts feeding on the grass of the glades; now he chased after them and again he flew past them; he lived on the roots of grasses and on the grass, on the fruit of the trees and on the mulberries of the thicket. He became a silvan man just as though devoted to the woods. For a whole summer after this, hidden like a wild animal, he remained buried in the woods, found by no one and forgetful of himself and of his kindred. But when the winter came and took away all the grass and the fruit of the trees and he had nothing to live on, he poured out the following lament in a wretched voice.

— Geoffrey of Monmouth, *Vita Merlini*

MYSTIC

The Mystic

The Mystic is a magician who has gone through the Occultist stage and usually aspects of the Man of Nature, and has stood on a threshold to make an informed choice. Instead of taking up the mantle of Leader, the Mystic adept instead chooses to pour all their energetic resources into lone mystical exploration.

The Mystic is often withdrawn from society, works deeply in the inner worlds, and carries energetic burdens connected to world-changing events where the creative patterns of the inner worlds are beginning to manifest in the outer world. The Mystic draws ever closer to personal union with the Divine, and their magical work facilitates this.

This card can indicate a time of introspection, meditation, and deep inner work that will widen the magician's understanding of the worlds, power, and Divinity itself. This can be a lonely time for a magician, as they will begin to realize that very few people around them share their level of understanding. Nor can their wisdom really be taught or shared: people have to find it out for themselves.

This card can also represent a man or woman who is deeply thoughtful, psychic, introverted, and magically empathic.

Mundane Divination: A thoughtful person who is a bit on the introverted side. They are best when left alone to get on with their life, and they are often searching for something in their life. It can appear when there is a need to withdraw and search deep within, to introspect, to turn away from the noise of daily life, and to search out what is meaningful.

MALE WARRIOR

Male Warrior

The image of the Male Warrior shows the bloodlust that can happen in battle. From a magician's perspective, it indicates that this male destructive power has completely taken over someone, who could themselves be male or female, and who will not stop their reign of destruction until they have accomplished everything they set out to do. This power has no reason behind it, so it cannot be reasoned with: it is a raw, killer instinct that will destroy everything in its path.

This card's appearance is a warning: either the magician is in danger of being destroyed by such a person, or there is the potential for that quality to rise in the male magician and consume them. It is a warning to temper some raw feelings of anger, some wish for revenge, or some wish to kill magically.

Bloodlust, a phenomenon well known in battle, can also release in magic, and the magician will destroy everything in their path if they do not keep it in check. Such power potential in humanity is normal; it is what we *do* with it that can turn it into something abnormal.

This card can also tell the magician that something is coming that may make them rage, but they should nevertheless keep their feelings in check: there is another way to deal with the issue that will not be so destructive for everybody—including themselves.

This card can also represent a destroying fire, which could be anything from a literal house fire to a powerful fever that could kill. It could be an inflammation that destroys, a power of fiery destruction, or a war that could wipe out everything in its path. The card should be read in context to the question. If the question is about health, then it indicates a raging infection or inflammation. If the question is about inner energy tides, then it warns of conflict, chaos, and destruction. The power's destructiveness depends on the range of the reading: if you are reading about world events, then this card can be devastating. If you are reading about a ritual action, then it warns that a power has come through that could turn your life, health, and magic upside down.

Mundane Divination: A fiery illness, a heated argument, a riot, destructive anger about to be unleashed.

Female Powers and Qualities

Note: The following five cards refer to generally female magical powers and qualities. But as with the previous section and for the same reasons, you should allow some fluidity in your divination.

ORACLE

The Oracle

The Oracle is a female occultist who is a magician, often with good psychic ability. Many women find their way to magic via their own natural psychic ability, usually through experimenting with tarot or other forms of divination. It can also represent a man with strong female intuitive qualities, who can draw on their deep psychic abilities.

The women (and men) whom the Oracle represents are ones studying or working within magic and the occult who rely a lot on their intuition. This card often represents younger female magicians in the early days of their magical lives. It can also indicate a female magician who relies too much on her natural instincts and psychic abilities, to the detriment of learning the art of magic itself.

The Oracle can also appear as an inner power, as an inner contact prompting the magician to look at something in divination. When the inner spirits and powers need to warn you of something or tell you something through divination, the Oracle can appear in readings. This appearance says, "you are not quite looking in the right direction; you need to ask different questions." If it appears regularly in readings, then it indicates that an inner contact is trying to connect with you and talk to you, but the two of you have not yet found the right way to communicate. The Oracle always wants to tell you something that you need to know.

Mundane Divination: This card can represent a psychic person in the reading. It can also represent a message that the person needs to hear.

PRIESTESS MAGICIAN

Priestess Magician

The Priestess Magician is a female occultist who is adept at her skills but expresses them through a mostly male-orientated magical system. Female adepts often get caught up in the 'masculine' control mentality that is so prevalent in Western magic, or else become shoehorned into a 'Scarlet Woman' role rather than simply being themselves as female magicians. Both are classic mistakes.

This card can indicate a female adept or initiate who is in danger of being typecast in a specific magical role or mindset that would ultimately stunt her magical growth. In some of the world's magical systems and groups, once women reach a certain stage of magical power they find themselves limited due to these outmoded systems having been originally designed by and for men. These systems were not often developed deliberately to keep women down; this was just how magic developed in the West. So this card can be a warning for a female magician to stay true to her own power.

This card can also represent a female magician who is a natural leader but has yet to take the deeper step into the shoes of the Hierophant. Once she relinquishes her need for control, the path to the Hierophant opens up and she can step into the new role. Of course, this card can appear for men or women, as with all the human cards: we have all these elements within us, and they can surface if we chose to let them.

If you are male and this card appears for you, and it is clear that it represents you and not a woman, then look deeply into how you are approaching your magic, and ensure that all elements of your personality have a balanced expression in your life and work.

Mundane Divination: This card can represent a strong and powerful woman, or a man with powerful feminine qualities, or it can represent that aspect of yourself. If it appears in your reading, then it can either a be a warning to ensure that such a personality is not getting out of control, or it can indicate that there is a need for that quality in your life path or actions.

FEMALE WARRIOR

Female Warrior

The Female Warrior is a complex power that can sometimes be difficult to understand depending on one's cultural programming. We often think of darkness and destruction as bad, but they are necessary for life to exist and are part of the balance of nature.

The Female Warrior is the light that shines out of intense darkness: she is the power of regenerative destruction as well as the warrior power that *confronts* degeneration, and the priestess who guards the Underworld.

Her power is drawn from the deep darkness and her mind is unemotional, cutting, and focused. When this card appears, it tells of a powerful priestess or magician who holds the power of the Limiter and who goes where most others would fear to tread.

The power of the Limiter, her sword, holds her bloodlust in check, and this is just as well: without that, her power can truly be terrifying.

This card represents a female magician with this warrior quality. She is at her best when guarding and defending, and at her worst when released to attack. She mediates the power of the destroying goddesses, and her magic will bring balance where there is imbalance—but often at a high price. When she appears in a reading, it indicates this female quality in the orbit of the situation, or that a female magician is about to go through the stage of the female warrior magician. It can also represent a time of struggle, where the qualities of the Female warrior, regardless of the gender of the reader, are needed. She appears when the magician needs to fight defensively within one's boundaries as opposed to fighting for conquest. She helps defend, she fights injustice, and she destroys chaos.

Mundane Divination: This card appears when one needs to fight, whether this is against an illness or an injustice, or to defend those who are defenceless. When she appears in a reading, pay close attention to where she appears: she could represent someone in the situation, a goddess power drawing close to assist you, or an aspect of yourself that needs to come out and fight.

HEALER

Healer

The Healer is a female natural magician and healer who brings the depths of the sea, an ancient power, into her surroundings. Her natural element is water, and regardless of the magic in which she is involved, her true skills lie in healing and regeneration.

The Healer is both happy and depressive, strong and yet needy: the nature of her power is water, and like water it flows through any available crack. She is at her best when her power and skills are allowed to find their own way; yet these powers are vulnerable to being dammed up inadvertently. Like the oceans, her depths are vast indeed, and yet her surface can be calm and still. Such a woman would not flourish under more constrained systems of magic, but left unfettered she can nourish everything around her.

For the magician, when this card appears in a reading, it can also represent goddess powers that rise out of the sea, a goddess of the waters. She is the goddess of the seas and rivers, a form of Yemaya who is a Mother to all. She can appear in readings either to represent a person or a power, an influence or an emotional state. She can appear when healing is triggered, and leaving her card out beside your bed when you are ill will draw her power to you.

Mundane Divination: This card appears when a person has started or is about to step into a healing process. She brings protection, healing, love, regeneration, and a deeper understanding of which emotional paths are best to tread.

SHAMANESS

Shamaness

The Shamaness is a female nature magician, the witch who tends the land, the woman who listens to the trees and the birds, who weaves her magic through instinct. Her skills lie in the winds, the rivers, the creatures, and the vast array of land and faery beings.

She is often not connected to more formal types of magic, but holds the remnants of the folk and faery magic from the land itself. She can bring balance to systems of magic that have become too constricted or have lost their connection with the world around them; yet her full commitment to such a system could restrict her too much. This card can also represent these aspects of nature magic in a female magician, when she puts her focus on the natural magic of the land.

This card reminds female magicians not to lose touch with the older powers of magic that run through the land, and that their power can be drawn from the land directly beneath their feet.

The Shamaness is also a mystic: she hears the utterances of Divinity on the winds, and it is through nature and magic that she finds her path deep into the inner worlds. Often this card can represent an older female magician who has integrated nature into her magical world, who is comfortable in her power, and who is a good teacher. Such a person is often overlooked, as they do not often appear powerful, but their force is hidden. When this card appears, a woman of this quality is involved in the situation or is within the situation's orbit. It can also indicate that some woman is coming to this stage of her magical development.

Mundane Divination: This card can represent a woman who is a force of nature, beholden to no one, and who is in touch with her natural surroundings. It can also represent the spirit of the wild nature woman trapped in a man's body, or a man with both male and female powers deeply embedded within them who has fully integrated them. The Shamaness is the wild woman who cannot easily be understood, who lives by the rules of nature rather than those of any specific culture.

Chapter IX

The Realm of Death and the Underworld

While I thought that I was learning how to live, I have been learning how to die.

— Leonardo da Vinci

The Realm of Death and the Underworld reaches deeply into the land, the Shallows of the Underworld, and the realm of the Rivers and Bridges of Death. Beyond these Shallows are the deeper aspects of the Underworld, which, while interesting, serve no real divinatory purpose.

The cards in this realm represent the areas where many magicians operate while working in the Underworld. They also offer hints for those adepts who wish to delve deeper into the Mysteries of the Justified Dead, ancient deities, and those trials that are often depicted in ancient funerary texts.

In divination, this realm is seen in terms of death and endings, deeper land contacts from the ancient past, and the ultimate function of the Underworld: the destruction of that which no longer has a purpose in the world of the living, which must be put into storage. The cards of this realm must be read both in relation to the work of the magician that they are undergoing, and also in the context of the question at hand. This realm is often ignored in divination, but it is ignored at our peril: if we do not understand whence the roots of our magic and lives spring, then our magic and lives are not anchored in the ancient and powerful land and powers that lie beneath us.

UNDERWORLD FOREST

Underworld Forest

M. P. 116

The vast Underworld comprises the inner remnants of our prehistoric landscape. It is also the realm that links the ancestral and faery realms to the Inner Desert, and to the Realm of Death. This card represents that aspect of the Underworld that is a junction point between the past, the dead, the dream worlds, and the place where the ancient powers of nature and ancestors meet. Beyond the Underworld Forest and its rivers lies the deeper Underworld, known to the Ancient Egyptians as the *Duat*, where the living magician undertakes the trials of the *Hours* and *Gates*: the trials of passing through the Underworld and emerging with the dawn sun.

The waters that flow around these ancient trees are the source of both the River of Death and the River of Dreams. It is a place where the spirits of the dead, the ancestors, the faery beings, and the ancient consciousnesses of primal forests flow together. As such, it is a place in the Underworld where humans, ancestors, and land beings can come together to work in greater service for the worlds around us.

The Underworld Forest is nature's equivalent of the Inner Library. All the wisdom and knowledge of the forest, creatures, faery/land beings, plants, and water is here in this vast, ancient place. When you need to learn about any of these things, this is where you go. In return for your learning, it is wise to offer service to this place, helping things settle as they pass into this place of hibernation.

When this card appears, it tells you that whatever magical process you are involved with has deep, unseen roots in the past and in the land. When this card appears, it offers you a chance to work in depth in vision with this place, to connect deeply with the spirits and beings that flow through it so that you can learn, grow, and help. It can also indicate the passing away from the surface world of some magic or power that is beginning to sink into the land in preparation for sleep.

The appearance of this card can indicate something passing into the past, going into storage or hibernation, and vanishing from the surface world. This is not a permanent state, but a 'station' through which power and beings can slowly pass as they descend into the Underworld. For magicians in particular, this card can indicate a need for them to go in vision into this Underworld place to work, or to go deeper into the Underworld to work in that part of the Underworld that is about evolution of the soul: the Hours and Gates, the Underworld Trial of the adept.

Mundane Divination: If this card appears in a mundane reading, then it can indicate some unhealthy influence in a situation. It can indicate past hidden agendas or old imbalances resurfacing, and in health readings it can indicate that the body is trying to process something that is unbalanced or even painful. It can indicate infection, hidden agendas, mental illness, or old unresolved issues playing a hidden part in a current situation. It has to be read in context to the question and situation, as its meanings are many and varied.

For forty days and forty nights
He wade through red blood to the knee,
And he saw neither sun not moon,
But heard the roaring of the sea.
O' they rode on and further on
Until they came to a garden green:
"Light down, light down, ye lady, free
Some of that fruit, let me pull for thee."
"O' no, o' no, true Thomas," she said to me,
"That fruit must not be touched by thee:
For all the plagues that are in hell
Light upon the fruit of this countrie.
But I have a loaf here in my lap
Likewise a bottle of wine,
And now, though we go farther on,
We'll rest a while, and ye may dine."
When he had eaten and drunk his fill,
"Lay down your head upon my knee,"
The lady said, "ere we climb yonder tree,
And I will show you fairies three.
O' see not ye yon narrow road
So thick beset wi' thorns and briars?
That is the path of righteousness,
Tho after it but few enquires.
And see not ye that broad broad road,
That lies across yon Lillie leven?
That is the path of wickedness,
Tho some call it the road to heaven.
And see not ye that bonnie road,
Which winds about the Fernie brae?
That is the road to fair Elfland,
Where you and I think night must gae.
But Thomas, ye must hold your tongue,
Whatever you may hear or see,
For gin a word you should chance to speak,
You will neer get back to your own countrie."
He has gotten a coat of the even cloth
And a pair of shoes of velvet green,
And till seven years were past and gone,
True Thomas on earth was never seen.

— Thomas the Rhymer,
True Thomas and the Queen of Elfland

BRIDGE OF DEATH

Bridge of Death

This card tells of a place and power in the inner Realm of Death. The Bridge of Death itself is an angelic being that we perceive in vision as a structure. It helps us cross the threshold from one world to another, be that into the Realm of Death/Rebirth, the inner worlds, or to the depths of Divinity.

This power is guarded by two angelic beings. They ensure that no one sets foot on the bridge unprepared, and that those who do make this step go wherever they are supposed to go.

This bridge spans the River of Death, and beyond it is the Inner Desert and entrance to the Realm of Death and the Underworld. Before we step forward to cross it, we are guided by its attendant angelic beings to pause and reflect. We are encouraged to reflect on our lives, to look at our actions in the full light of truth, and to be willing to learn from our deeds.

The dead cross this bridge. At times, so can living magicians who wish to work in the Underworld Realm of Death. This is the bridge that leads to the realm depicted in the Egyptian *Book of Gates*.

When this card appears in a magical reading, it can have a variety of possible meanings. The first is literal and indicates, depending on its position, that the reader as a magician will be working at the threshold of death in service. This could mean escorting someone through the death process, or being a presence at the bridge during a time of disaster when there are many dead. Rather than plan such work, the magician often finds themselves pulled into sleep or deep meditation only to discover themselves working at the edge of death.

The other thing this card could indicate is its more abstract, overall dynamic: a time for deep reflection, inner examination, and self-truth. The magician or subject of the reading has come to some threshold, and a retreat is impossible. They must therefore think very carefully about how to move forward. It indicates a need to reassess one's attitudes and actions, and to atone for past mistakes, stupid actions, and immature behaviour.

This card's appearance also indicates that the magician has come to a threshold in their magical world, and they have the option to step forward into deep, unknown territory. First they must be sure that they are fully aware of who and what they are—hence the necessity of self-examination. Once this awareness is reached, then it is time to step off the cliff into untrodden magical territory. Such a step is an early preparation for crossing the Abyss.

This card can also indicate that the subject of reading is coming to the end of something major in their lives, that they are about to take a step that will lead them into powerfully unknown territory. It can also indicate that an ill or old person is preparing for death.

Mundane Divination: The appearance of this card, besides the above descriptions, can also mean that a course of action, if continued, will bring about the permanent end of something. It is a threshold that *can* be drawn back from if the way ahead is destructive; or it may herald the end of a bad situation. It often indicates the way ahead for such an ending, depending on where it falls in a reading, and it gives the reader the choice either to continue with some course of action, or withdraw.

Wandering through the building I find myself gravitating to the main door, passing by the beautiful works of art upon the walls of the hall—depictions and patterns that seem to be a part of me and to tell my story. How strange that they should be so familiar to me, so like me, and so of me.

Something has settled within me and I can feel the end of the tunnel. I truly thank heaven for Aaron, for giving me a chance to find help, to find sanctuary from the battle that rages within and all around me. I know I will have to gather myself at some point and leave this wondrous sanctuary, but it feels like it has become my home, my life and my whole reality: how much can change in the course of a few days.

I open the door to greet the afternoon sun and feel his warm winds upon my face. But the door stands open and before me is mist—nothing but a thick silent and empty fog that obscures the nothing beyond it. My heart freezes in terror: I know, in a deep ancient magical knowing, that there is nothing beyond the door. The world beyond has gone and has no place for me, no meaning, no path and no future. Fear holds my throat fast, like a noose, pulled hard. I close the door but not in defeat, but with a grim determination.

— Josephine McCarthy, *The Last Scabbard*

DEATH

Death

This card indicates the final end of something. It can be the death of a person, a life cycle, or an era; or the end of something that will not be revisited. Besides the literal expression of this card as the death of someone, it can also indicate surrendering something that no longer has a place in the physical world.

It is the end of substance, the smashing of the vessel, and the release of the eternal spirit or energy; and it is the acceptance of an ending, a completion. We avoid and sometimes fear death in all its forms, yet it is a normal process for a spirit to shed the old skin and step into the new.

Endings happen around us all the time and we do not perceive them as 'death'; but when we are confronted by the death card, it can trigger an almost primal fear. This is a normal and natural survival mechanism. This card can appear to a magician when they are permanently leaving behind an old system of work that will not be revisited, or leaving some area to which they will never return. It is a final ending, anything from a physical death to the irreparable breakdown of a car. Once the reader realizes this, then the card can be used to measure the lifespan of a future event, or to see when the end of some cycle will come.

Mundane Divination: An end, a full stop to something, regardless of what it is. At a stretch, when a reading is looking at seasons or phases of time, this card can represent winter, when the plants die back.

DESTRUCTION

Destruction

This card represents the powers and beings that flow through, and with, destruction. In a Tarot deck, the Tower represents destruction. In this deck, we look at the beings and powers *behind* the destruction, as well as the destruction itself.

This card tells us about energies and beings that trigger destruction in all its glorious forms. When it appears in a reading, it warns that the magician is in the orbit of some destructive power, or that their current path may be leading them to destruction, and they need to reconsider their actions.

Destruction is natural and its lessons are important to learn, but unnecessary destruction is something magicians can—and do—avoid wherever possible.

The level of destruction involved depends on the question and the card's position. The card can represent anything from destruction clearing the way for something new and better (loss of job, loss of home, crashing the car but being okay), to a major pulse of destructive power seeking a vessel to fill, or a catastrophe. When this card appears, the magician needs to check for any weak spots in their work or actions that could precipitate a destructive incident. Then they can look to see if some magical action should be taken to avoid a destructive pulse.

This card should never be ignored: to do so will likely bring a destructive event into your life. If it appears prominently in the reading, then do a yes/no reading to pinpoint exactly where in your life the destruction may manifest.

Mundane Divination: A difficult event or energy may trigger an ending to a situation. It can also represent a great deal of pain, a destructive event, or a serious stage in an illness. It can be a frightening card, but it must also be viewed in context. It is also always wise to remember that often destruction has to occur before new ground can be trodden. Our lives are often a series of 'mini deaths' and destructive events that serve to push us further along the path of evolving and growing. If this card appears in a mundane reading, then question your motives and choices: it may be better to make different plans, change your course of action, or plan for tough times ahead.

Sometimes—most times—destruction can be avoided by sensible decisions. But sometimes you have simply to take a deep breath and walk your way through it, one foot at a time. Once you come out the other end of such a destructive phase then the Star father will appear, bringing new seeds, new pathways, new potentials, and new beginnings.

Chapter X

Layouts

Most people, including ourselves, live in a world of relative ignorance. We are even comfortable with that ignorance, because it is all we know. When we first start facing truth, the process may be frightening, and many people run back to their old lives. But if you continue to seek truth, you will eventually be able to handle it better. In fact, you want more! It's true that many people around you now may think you are weird or even a danger to society, but you don't care. Once you've tasted the truth, you won't ever want to go back to being ignorant.

— Socrates

Layout Choice and
Interpreting Your Readings

The correct choice and use of a layout is critical to a reading's accuracy, particularly a magical one where you need more detail. You should be very specific about the meaning of each position in a layout, as this pays huge dividends when it comes to interpreting the combined meaning of each position and the card that falls in it. When a position is the 'home' of a particular card, then you read the position card and the card that falls in that position together. When a layout position card falls in another part of a layout, then you can read the two layout positions, and the two working cards that fall in those positions, together. If you can make use of this sort of 'grammar,' then the deck can speak to you in more depth.

Again, the meanings of the layout positions must be specific in order to obtain accurate results. Once you have mastered reading in this way, you will slowly learn to design your own layouts so that you can take readings specifically tailored to your areas of interest.

In this chapter we will look at four layouts that give you different ways to look at a situation. Each layout has a particular function, and you can use any or all of them depending on what information you need. The four layouts are the Foundation/Mystical Map, the Landscape layout (which is an abridged version of the Mystical Map), the Tree of Life layout, and a Directional layout.

It is wise to keep a journal of important or specific readings so that you can go back to them in retrospect and truly draw understanding from the cards. Hindsight is the finest teacher in divination. Over time you will start to see patterns of behaviour in the cards, and where certain cards appear for certain meanings and situations. Looking back over readings after an event, you will see how the voices were telling you what was coming, in their own way. Then you will develop a true knowledge of the cards, one far more valuable than mere book learning, especially when drawn from those books which analyse the cards from a psychological perspective. The cards are a vocabulary for your own inner voice, and for the voices of the contacts around you.

However, be warned—and this warning is pertinent for all magical readings—if you are emotionally invested in a particular reading, then you run the risk of attracting inner parasites who will try to play with you by giving you false readings. It is something that happens to most magical readers at one time or another, and when you spot it, then it is time to cleanse the cards (use incense smoke or dry salt) and put them away for a while. This allows the links to the parasites to die back: it literally starves them out. It is a lesson that is well learned, and will teach you always to approach readings without emotions, as emotions are the food of such beings.

Foundation/Mystical Map Layout

The Foundation/Mystical Map layout is exactly what the name suggests: it is an extensive layout that gives the reader insight into the deeper powers that run through the whole life and death of the magician. It shows the deep foundational powers, dynamics, fate, and deeper reasons why you chose to come into your current life. It is what your life and work is all about in terms of your soul's evolution, its service, and your unique expression in this life. It is not a layout you would use often, but it can give strong insights into the currents of power that flow, hidden away, beneath the surface of everyday life. It is not about who you marry, where you work, or anything like that: it is about the fate patterns of creation and destruction that run throughout your life as your deeper spirit seeks to express itself.

For a non-magical person, this reading can be terrifying, as this deck pulls no punches: it is specific and to the point. However, for a magician who is aware that the dynamics of creation and destruction flow in equal amounts through the life of an aspiring adept, it can give major insights into why the twists and turns of their own fate express as they do, both in their magical and daily life. Gaining insight into the deeper currents that flow around them can help a magician walk through the destructive aspects of their lives, knowing why they are there and that they are serving a purpose. It can also help them understand and work more closely with the creative aspects of their lives, by revealing which beings and powers are seeking expression and connection with them.

So if you are not on a magical or mystical path, then it might be an idea to avoid using this foundation layout unless you want to terrify yourself!

Foundation/Mystical Map Layout

I The Mother Earth

This is ground zero for the reading. It can mean the human body if the reading is about a person, or it can mean the land beneath where a person lives, or the land that a reading is about. *Mother Earth* is the vessel, the body, the completion of creation. It is a 'now' position: it tells you about ground zero at the present time of the reading. The position tells of the energy, health, and state of the 'vessel' at the centre of the reading.

II Union

This tells you about the relationships with the subject or person that are important. If the reading is about a person, then it tells you about the strongest interaction the person is having that is affecting them, for good or bad. It can indicate a person with whom they have a powerful relationship, it can show agreements or contracts with which they are heavily involved, or it can indicate a power or being with which they are interacting.

III Star Father

This position is the long-term future. It shows what is forming in a particular fate pattern and tells you the long-term pattern that will come to pass, if the road walked continues. This is a very important position for magicians to look at when they are using this layout. It corresponds to the magical direction of south/future/up, and shows the longer-range, long-term future consequences, for good or bad, of the path currently being followed.

IV The Abyss

This is the position that shows what is deep in the Underworld which has passed and will never return. It is the past, the magical direction of north/down. If the reading is about a place then it can show what is deeply buried beneath it. The card that falls in the position of the Abyss is deep in the past and cannot be revived. It is related to the Underworld.

V The Gate

Things that appear in this position are falling away from a person or situation. But a gate is always a two-way thing: whatever is indicated here can return, pause on the threshold, or continue its journey into the past (which will take it down into the Underworld).

VI Temple of Ancestors

This position indicates what influence or contact is flowing from the reader's deep ancestral line, or from local ancestors in the land, or from ancestral priesthoods. This is the position in the layout where the ancestors speak to us, advise us, or let themselves be known. This position can also indicate inherited skills and gifts. This position is related to the Blood Ancestor, the Foundation, and the River of Dreams.

VII Inner Temple

The card that appears in this position shows us the deeper, more profound magical or inner aspects affecting a person or the subject. It can also show us the deeper mystical aspects of a person, place, or thing. This is also the position of inner contacts, angelic beings, and deities. The Inner Temple is removed from most of humanity, and is found only through magical or mystical development. It is the anchor and root behind mystical aspects of religion, behind mystical magical lines and systems; and it is from here that all magical and religious temples take their inner, most purest form. What appears in this position should be read in this context. This position is related to the Inner Companion, the Inner Librarian, Hidden Knowledge, and the Spirit Guide.

VIII Blood Ancestor

Just as the Inner Temple is the deep threshold in the inner realms, the Blood Ancestor position tells of the deepest ancestral connection the subject has in the Underworld. The card that lands here tells you of an ancient or root blood ancestor, what gifts or problems they have passed directly to you, and what relevance that bloodline has to you. The card that falls in this position can also indicate if any ancestral line is particularly active or problematic, depending on the question. It can also indicate magical work in the deep Underworld with the assistance of your own ancestors.

IX Foundation

This position shows the deep anchor of a person or subject. It is what has happened in the past that will deeply influence the future. Anything holding a person or situation back due to past life events or ancestral influences will show in this position. Similarly, anything that laid the foundation for a fate pattern within which the subject is now active will show here. It is the deep roots of the present that will determine how the future unfolds. Whatever appears in this position cannot be changed but must be incorporated into the future, whether the card that falls here is good or bad. It is the foundation upon which you stand; and if it is a weak foundation, then knowing that will help you compensate, counterbalance, and transform that weakness into a strength.

X Weaver of Creation

This position tells of the fate patterns of the subject. This is the position of the fate pattern within which we are currently immersed, which could be a long-term fate pattern or a short-term one. It can indicate whether or not we are in harmony with our current fate pattern, and the card that falls in this position tells us the overall theme of that fate pattern. The card that falls in this position is directly related to the card that falls in Foundation: what happened in the past defines how we engage with our current fate path, and both positions can be interpreted together get the most possible information out of the reading. This position is related to the Three Fates, the Wheel of Fate, and the Chariot.

XI Grindstone

This position tells of what is limiting us that must be overcome. These limitations and difficulties grind us and polish us to make us stronger. This is a position of hard work that brings great success, of learning that may be difficult but which will be worth it in the end. This position is related to the Keeper of Justice and the Challenge of the Gods.

XII Magical Temple

This position shows what is happening in our magical lives. It shows what powers are manifesting in our magical work, and can also show any interference or issues with our magical path or magical actions. It also shows magical temples whose orbit the magician may be in, and the card that falls in this position shows what is flowing to the subject from these magical temples. If the subject of the reading is involved in a particular religion, then it can also be a position for the energetic egregore of that religion, i.e. what energetically flows to the subject from that religion. This position is related to the Threshold Keeper.

XIII Home and Hearth

This is the position of home and hearth. It is the family, the tribe, the local community, the family home...it all depends on your subject matter and question, but this position is always about the outer world around the subject. It is mundane, day-to-day living and the environment in which that day-to-day living is done.

XIV The Unraveller

This position tells of something that is being unravelled and prepared to pass into the past, through the Gate. Any situation that has reached its peak and is now unravelling in order to break up and compost will appear in this position. Whatever lands in this position is passing away from the subject and no longer has a strong place in the subject's life. This card is related to the Underworld.

XV River of Dreams

This is the place of sleep and dreams, of visions and night times. Whatever is happening in the sleep, dreams, or visions of a person will show here. If something powerful appears here, see what is in the Weaver of Creation, the Ancestral Temple, or the Inner Temple positions. This will tell you where the power of the dream is coming from, which in turn will tell you what could be happening. This position is related to the Utterer, the Underworld, and Premonition.

XVI The Path of Hercules

This is the path forward: the Path of Hercules. It tells of the short-term future and is aligned to the directions of east and south. Whereas south/up is a long-term formation, east-flowing-south tells of the future that is already on its way, that has formed, and that is unrolling itself into action. This also shows where the subject matter is going in terms of what will happen next as a direct result of the action in the rest of the reading. In the mystical map reading, it will tell of the life ahead for the subject.

Only sacred divination united with the gods truly gives a share in the divine life, participating in foreknowledge and divine thoughts, and truly makes us divine.

— Iamblichus (c. A.D. 250–330)

Landscape Layout

The landscape layout is an abridged version of the Mystical Map layout and can be used far more often, and in different ways. It can be used for mundane readings to get an overview of a situation, or it can be used for specific magical questions that look at situations, possibilities, people, places, and things. It will show what dynamics are at play, in both the inner and physical worlds, and it will also show how fate paths unfold as a result of a decision. Because of its reach, it can be used to look at variables and alternatives, and to see how power and magic would unfold in the future if a certain action is taken. It can also show what powers and influences are around a land area, building, person, or magical object. It can be used, for example, to answer a question which has the form: "If I do X, what will happen in the short-term and also long-term future?" This can be important to a magician, as sometimes the short-term results from an action can look good, but there may be disastrous long-term consequences. This layout lets you to check both ends of this spectrum at once.

It is also a map of a person's *inner landscape*. As a magician gets deeper into their training, they become aware of an inner template of power that feeds into their lives and also composts things out of their life. This layout tracks the movement in and out of such dynamics in their inner landscape, which eventually feeds into their outer life.

As you will see from the layout's illustration, a couple of the positions use different base cards to the Mystical Map. This is both to make the layout better for more frequent use, and to enable you to combine both meanings of a position. And if you feel better interpreting the card using the meaning of the position in the Mystical Map layout, then do so: both are valid options.

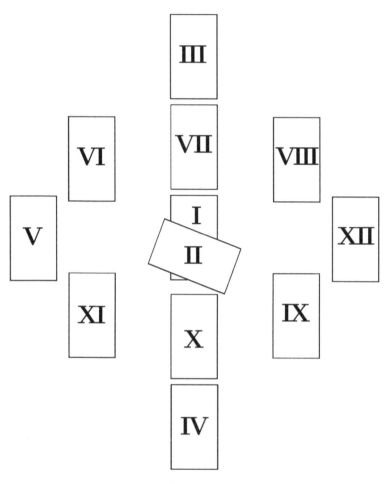

Landscape Layout

I Mother Earth

The body, land, subject of the reading.

II Union

What the subject is having a relationship with. This can be a person, power, substance, energy, or object depending on the question asked.

III Star Father

The long term future of the subject if they continue on their chosen current path. This card, and how it changes with the question, will show you the long-term outcome of whatever has been posed in the question.

IV Abyss

What is in the deep past, which has now gone.

V Gate

What is in the past that may have relevance for the future, or what is passing away to eventually descend into the Abyss.

VI Wheel of Fate

In this layout, this position is the Weaver of Fate, *she who weaves the threads of the future*. The Wheel of Fate is the inner power that brings the various changes of short-term fate patterns and shifts them according to the subject's actions and choices. Having the Wheel in this position makes it easier to spot current patterns and phases that the subject is going through. Choices can change this pattern, and the card that falls in this position can indicate, if for example, the subject is making silly or unwise choices.

VII Grindstone

This position, and the card that falls upon it, represents the difficulties that must be overcome on the current fate path.

VIII Inner Temple

Here, this position can stand for both the Magical Temple and the Inner Temple. It shows what is flowing into the physical world of the subject from the inner worlds.

IX Home and Hearth

Just as in the Mystical Map layout, the Home and Hearth is the home, family, or tribe.

X Unraveller

What is being unravelled in the subject or is falling away from the subject. Whatever falls in this position is being dismantled in order for it to fall away from the life of the subject.

XI River of Dreams

This is the position of the subject's sleep, dreams, and also visions or visionary work.

XII Path of Hercules

The Path of Hercules is the subject's short-term future and path forward if they continue on their chosen path.

Tree of Life Layout

The Tree of Life layout can be used in various ways, and it is an incredibly flexible layout to work with. There are two basic ways you can work with it. The first way, which relies on the layout's deeper aspect, is to work with the positions in the same way one works with the Mystical Map layout or the Landscape layout, where each position has its own 'home' card.

The second way adopts a more mundane approach, and this can be used to gain yes-or-no answers, as well as a more focused view on what is happening or will happen to a situation, place, or person.

Tree of Life Layout

The deeper approach

This way of approaching the Tree of Life layout would be used for magical and mystical readings. Each position has its root power identity, and the cards that fall in these positions should be read in conjunction with the root power meaning. This layout can be used to look at a specific person or situation, and see what deeper powers are at play, without getting too much information that can 'swamp' the reading.

For example, say you wish to look at the suitability of a building or patch of land for the construction of a magical temple. By using this deeper approach to the Tree of Life layout, you can see exactly what deeper powers are flowing through the space: the deeper powers tend not to change much over time. The more superficial energies, which can change frequently, could then be ascertained by using the second approach to the Tree of Life layout.

You can also use this approach to reflect on the deeper powers flowing through your life and your current path through fate, or to look at active and longer-term magical patterns. It is not much use for more mundane readings, for which you would use the second, more mundane method.

Key Words

Here are key words that the magician can use for the deeper Tree of Life layout:

Star Father I Beginnings, conception, the Word, what flows out of magical east, what is flowing from the inner worlds and coming into manifestation.

Keeper of Time II Giving shape, giving a time span, the inclusion of time and fate. What deep power has triggered for fate to express itself.

Holder of Light III What is being held back, is in hibernation, or is withdrawn.

Light Bearer IV The path builder, the Opener of the Way.

Imprisoner V Necessary restriction, what is held back that enables to way to be open.

Pure Balance VI The fulcrum, the power that holds the balance, which allows the fate to express.

Grindstone VII Difficulty that develops the subject, hardship that strengthens, boundaries, control, physical difficulty, physical patterns of fate.

Unraveller VIII Ease that can undo the subject, loosening that potentially weakens, loss of boundaries, lack of control, mental or magical difficulties.

Threshold Guardian IX Creativity, inner vision, inner landscape, what is the inner bridge that allows the inner powers to flow to the outer, physical subject.

Mother Earth X The body, the land, the outcome, the completion of the beginning, coming to fruit.

Positions one, two, and three should be read together as an overview of the question or situation. Four, five, and six should be read as the deeper powers that are active in the story. Position four and position seven are related to each other: what power position four brings to a subject, is processed through position seven (the seventh and seven are always key magical indicators). Position five and position eight are also related to each other: if the lessons indicated in position eight are not learned, then the power of position five will spring into action to restrict something out of circulation.

Position one, six, nine, and ten are like a highway that power can flow up or down. In divination we usually look at the downward flow from conception (1) to completion (10). It is the middle pillar or axis of power, and the positions on either side of the axis create tensions and oppositions that allow the power to continue to flow.

As you can see, the position meanings are deep and magical, and much can be drawn from a reading using this method if you take the time to meditate upon it; but it is not much good for more mundane or simple questions.

The simpler approach

This method of interpretation is simpler, self-explanatory (use the key words on each card in the illustration on the opposite page), and much better for mundane readings and simple yes-or-no questions. The final position, position ten, is the answer to the question, and the preceding cards tell you how that answer comes about. The illustration of this layout gives you the numbered sequence and tells you what each position stands for.

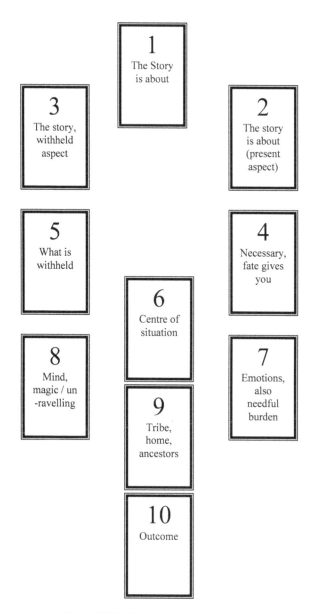

Tree of Life Layout: simpler approach

Layout of the Four Directions

This six-card layout looks at the subject, what influences flow from each direction, and finally, what is interacting with the subject. It is a very versatile layout and can be used to look at a person, situation, or place, depending on the question and how you use the key words.

The key words in each direction are related to each other, and you work with the most relevant key words depending on the subject matter of the reading and your question. First we will look at the layout pattern itself and the key words for each position, and then we will discuss how these should be interpreted in a reading.

1. **Centre:** The body, a place, the land, a person, an object. This position tells you about the subject of the reading.

2. **East:** Coming into being, potential, air, utterance, spring, incoming, learning.

3. **South:** The path ahead, the future, fire, summer, work.

4. **West:** Family, home, ageing, water, autumn, falling away, legacy.

5. **North:** Ancestors, death, the past, winter, earth.

6. **Union:** The biggest influence on the subject, relationships, input.

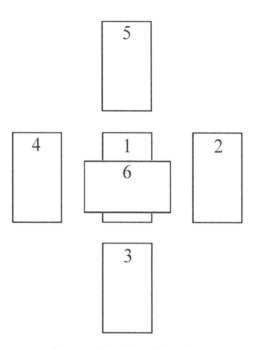

Layout of the Four Directions

Different uses of this layout

How you approach the positions and key words depends very much on what sort of question you are asking. This is a simple layout, and therefore good for simple magical or mundane readings; and it can be used to pinpoint the timing of something, the influences of something, or the energies of a space in the various directions. It can be used to see what outer influences are flowing into a person's life, as well as what inner or magical energies are affecting them.

Here are some examples of approaches and uses of key words:

Checking a space:

Using the directional attributes, you can do a reading for a house or property, and look at the different energies flowing into and around it. You would not use any of the key words; simply use the direction and the card that falls in that direction. The central card is the overall property, and the last card tells you how the people who live in it affect it.

If a negative or destructive card fell in the south, you would then need to look a bit closer at the south part of the property. First you would want to know if the danger was inner or outer, which you can establish by your next question: "show me the inner energies in the south of this property." Using the same layout, you can use the key words to look at what is coming into the south, what its path ahead is, what is falling away, and so forth. You can then do the same for the physical aspect of the building.

Checking energies and magic flowing around a person:

You would use the directions in a magical sense in conjunction with the key words that define time. So, for example, position two would use the key words 'east' (magical utterance or magical systems of air) and 'incoming'. Whatever card falls in this position tells you the health (or otherwise) of the energies of 'east,' 'utterance,' and 'beginnings' around the person. The south tells of fire energies, magic, and the future path, the west of emotional or water energies and what is fading into the past, and so forth.

Checking the potential success of something

For example, "If I do X, will my project be successful?" Here, position two would be the idea forming, position three would be future, position four would be its 'harvest' (what legacy does it leave?), position five would tell you what is already in the past to do with the question, and the final card will tell you about the people or powers you would deal with or otherwise interact with in your project.

As you can see, the four-directional layout is very flexible, and is basically defined by what you are looking at, how you ask the question, and where your focus is. Different card readers can develop their own unique way of working with this layout. To get started with this layout, you could just use the basic pattern of east/beginning, south/future, west/fading, and north/past. You can then gradually add other attributes and meanings as you gain confidence.

Final Advice

What makes a reading successful and clear to read is the layout, and your focus and intent when you ask your question. If you are not very clear in your mind about what you are asking, then the answer will be similarly confused and vague. Ensure that you know the layout you are using, shuffle the cards well, and keep your focus on the specific question.

Ensure that the question you ask has boundaries. If, for example, you ask something vague like "show me my future," then the cards will either show you the next big event coming in your life—which could be the next day, the next year, or in a decade's time—or they may simply show you your death: the ultimate future for us all.

It is better to be clear and specific, and this will also help you focus your mind on what you feel you need to know. Never try to stretch beyond what is necessary; just focus on the task at hand.

To return to the example, if you need to know what is happening in the next six months so that you can plan accordingly, then be clear about that. Your question would be, "show me my life over the next six months." If you do not need to know the overall picture of your life, but just want to look at a specific area of it, then define that, too: "show me my magical life over the next six months," "show me my life at work over the next six months," and so on.

Many people when they first begin to use divination can end up acting like a child in a candy shop if they are not careful. You should use divination wisely, to look at things that you really need to look at.

It is also possible to *over-read* a situation. When you first do a reading about something, you will get a fairly broad, long-term overview of the event or subject. If you then continuously do readings on the same subject, you can end up shortening the timeline you are looking at: it gets closer and closer in the more you continue to look at the same situation. So use your common sense.

In terms of energy hygiene, when you have finished doing some readings, go and wash your hands with soap and some dry salt. This will strip away any energy resonance from your hands. This is particularly important when the reading is a difficult one. If the deck feels energetically dirty or sticky after a bad reading, then lay it out on a tea-towel, pour on some dry salt, and give it a good salt rub. Then wrap it up in the salty tea-towel and leave it to sit for an hour or so. Afterwards, shake and brush the salt off the deck. Alternatively you can smudge the deck with frankincense smoke.

Above all, enjoy playing with the deck and learning about, experimenting with, and getting to know its individual powers and personalities!

Ingram Content Group UK Ltd.
Milton Keynes UK
UKHW051307040623
422848UK00015B/74